THE KINDNESS CODE

SIMPLE ACTS - EXTRAORDINARY RESULTS. TO CHANGE YOUR LIFE & MAYBE THE WORLD.

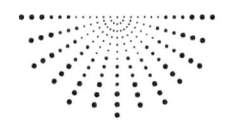

HARSHA LIYANAGE PH.D., MBA.

October 2020.

ISBN: 9798695733549

Copyright © Harsha Liyanage. All rights reserved.

For any inquiries regarding this book, please email:

Kindnesscode@gmail.com

No part of this book may be reproduced in any form or by any electronic or mechanical means, including information storage and retrieval systems, without written permission from the author, except for the use of brief quotations in a book review.

EDITORIAL REVIEWS

Heart-warming and enthralling book, draws the reader gently into the Kindness Code, with its two principles and three steps. During a time of great darkness, it serves as a candle to light the pathway to a better world.

— PROF. TIM UNWIN, AUTHOR AND UNESCO CHAIR (UK).

In this wonderful book, Harsha Liyanage helps us understand the art and value of being kind to ourselves and others, using a language that is easy to appreciate and drawing on his life's experience and deep wisdom.

— TORBJÖRN FREDRIKSSON, AUTHOR, UNCTAD (GENEVA).

This book is an interesting read to build hopes at a time of chaos. Very important and timely book.

— DR. SHARIFF ABDULLAH, AUTHOR AND ADVOCATE FOR SOCIETAL TRANSFORMATION, COMMONWAY INSTITUTE (USA).

Harsha takes us down his memory lane to make the reader decode the Kindness Code. It is a magical pill, and a simple cure to a burdensome heart.

— BINESH TOOR, AVID READER AND SOCIAL
MEDIA ACTIVIST (PAKISTAN).

Kindness Code is concise, simple, and a practical guide to a kinder planet. The author, in his expressive style, has beautifully cracked the code of 'random acts of kindness' to show us the way to be more kind to ourselves and to the others.

— MADU RATNAYAKE, AVID READER AND
GENERAL MANAGER, VIRTUSA (SRI LANKA).

Reading the Kindness Code reminded me of the wise and calm Harsha Liyanage I met over 10 years ago working on internet projects in Sri Lanka. Whether speaking one on one or talking to a crowd of hundreds, Harsha always emanated light and kindness. It was infectious, enlivening and, ultimately, highly productive. The book gives this same feeling. It is welcome tool and guide for these odd times.

— MARK SURMAN, AUTHOR AND EXECUTIVE
DIRECTOR, MOZILLA FOUNDATION (CANADA).

CONTENTS

About the Book   ix
About the Author   xi

1. Fragile Grip on Reality — 1
2. Kindness - the Heavenly Splendor — 5
3. The Beast — 9
4. Kindness Code — 13
   Ignite — 19
5. Ignite Kindness with Positive Imagination — 21
6. Mother Nature is Heavenly — 23
7. The River Flows with Happiness — 25
8. Cherry Blossoms and Smiles — 27
9. Hills in the Mist Infuses Positive Vibes — 31
10. Beach: Escorting Waves of Hopes — 33
11. Sunshine Sparks Happiness — 37
12. Wildflower Meadows are Tendering — 41
13. Puppy is Dancing — 45
14. Positive Quotes to Ignite Kindness — 47
15. Chemistry — 51
   Light-up — 55
16. Be-Kind-to-You-First — 57
17. Express Your Love (Better) — 61
18. It is Okay to be Vulnerable — 65
19. The Worst Truth is Better Than the Sweetest Lie — 69
20. Kindness Without Confronting Ego — 73
21. Managing Conflicts in Relationships — 75
22. Fail Successfully — 79
23. Dare to Dream — 83
24. Law of Attraction — 87
   Radiate — 91
25. Radiate Kindness — 93
26. Ant & Me: Love & Kindness — 97

27. Meeting with a Terrorist Leader	101
28. Kind Strangers in the Global Village	105
29. Kindness as a Way of Life	109
30. Mindfulness	113
31. Death	117
32. Self-transcendence	121
33. Meditation	127
34. Why Kindness Code?	129
Acknowledgments	133
Bibliography	135
One Final Word	137

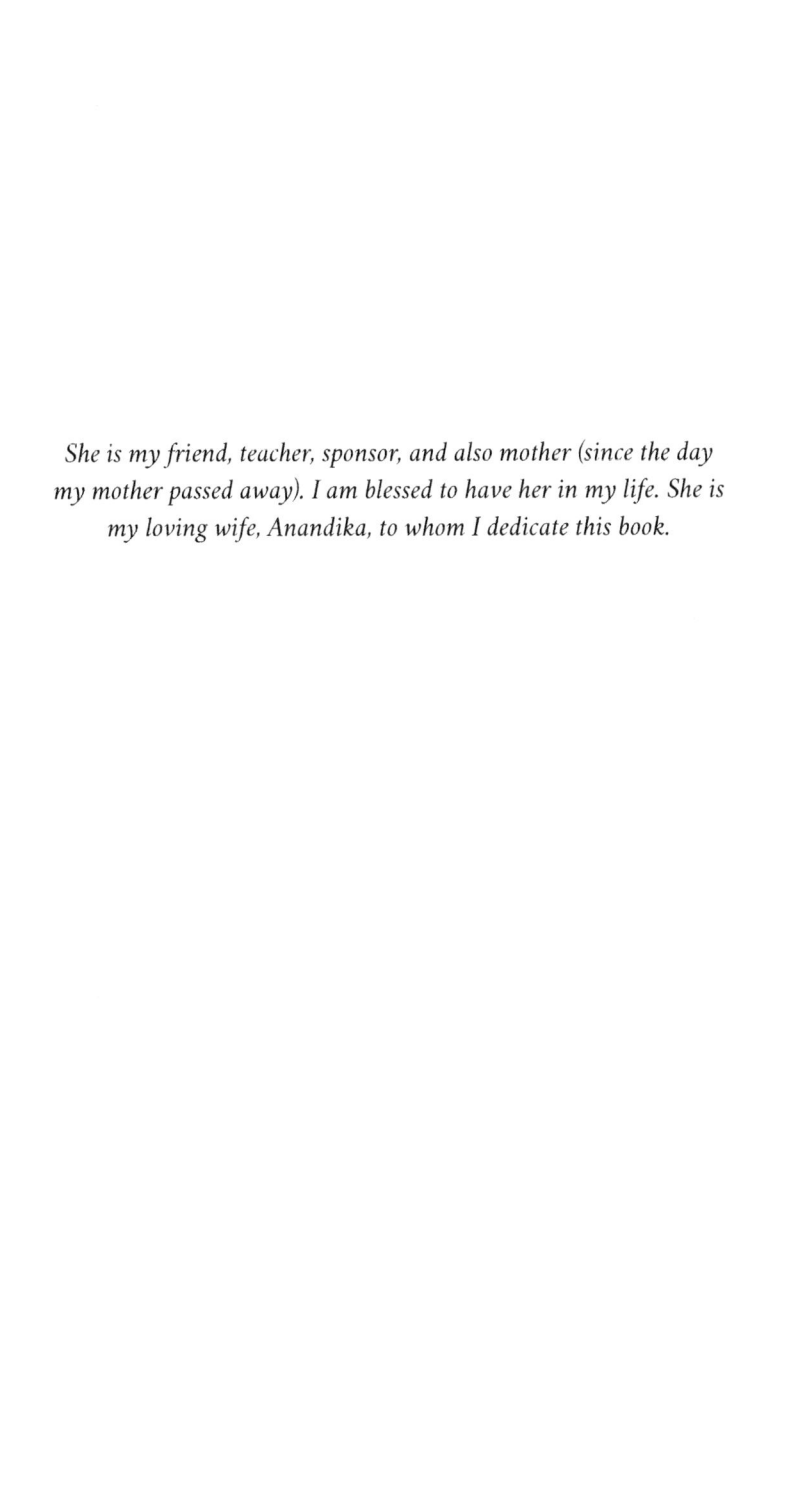

She is my friend, teacher, sponsor, and also mother (since the day my mother passed away). I am blessed to have her in my life. She is my loving wife, Anandika, to whom I dedicate this book.

ABOUT THE BOOK

Kindness is a universal language, bringing harmony to ease the tensions in our world. This book is a creative piece of art. It presents a way to use kindness as an active ingredient to live a happy, dynamic, and successful life, in which you can then find a higher purpose.

If you are passionate about ethical living, health and well-being, meditation, and mindfulness, this publication is a gift designed for you.

The concept of loving-kindness, introduced in Buddhism, has been adapted, integrating aspects of science and human behavior to derive the Kindness Code.

The Kindness Code, introduced in the book, is a simple three-step guide to show you how to draw upon the positive energy of loving-kindness from the world around you and deepen your happiness and productivity.

Through the use of stories, this book will guide you to become a better version of yourself and will lead you to discover a higher purpose.

The author derived most stories from personal encounters. Some experiences have been reconstructed to maintain clarity and readability. Character names are not reflective of any individual.

For more kindness updates please visit:
www.KindnessCode.org

- twitter.com/KindnessCode
- facebook.com/KindnessCode.co
- instagram.com/kindness_code

ABOUT THE AUTHOR

Harsha Liyanage is an internationally recognized humanitarian activist.

Born on the beautiful island of Sri Lanka, Harsha has been exposed to meditation practices since childhood. He has adopted kindness as a way of life due to growing up inside a brutal civil war while facing poverty.

Harsha studied biotechnology to receive a Ph.D. as a Japanese Government Scholar and served as an international consultant at the United Nations in Geneva. His social innovations have resulted from Peace Meditations during the ethnic war, to sustainable social enterprises to empower impoverished communities. He founded Sarvodaya-Fusion, a social enterprise to help the poor, and co-founded Grasshoppers.lk as a for-profit venture.

International Development Research Centre (IDRC) of Canada has awarded a Fellowship to Harsha, recognizing his social innovations in Sri Lanka and supported expansion in Asia and Africa. Harsha lives in the United Kingdom with wife Anandika and their three daughters, Devni, Savani, and Asini.

linkedin.com/in/harshaliyanage
twitter.com/KindnessCode
facebook.com/smilingharsha

My religion is very simple. My religion is kindness.

— HIS HOLINESS THE DALAI LAMA

1
FRAGILE GRIP ON REALITY

Silent but electric. His menacing red eyes locked onto mine. He had a grip of steel, yet I felt the tightness of his hand weakening in response to my peacefulness. A sense of victory coursed through me; my compassion leapt into action.

Moments ago, the very same man tried to kill my sister.

"Help, help; this man is going to kill me! He won't stop chasing me…"

Her screaming voice trailed off on the other end of the phone, and my heart dropped. She had only left our car moments before to stop by her colleague's house briefly. Darkness was falling. The electricity was about to cut out at any moment. We were experiencing a daily two-hour power cut due to a severe drought in the country.

I was waiting with my three young daughters, who were playing in the back seat, unaware of the situation at hand.

I was weaponless, but I had one thing I could find solace in - a mind I had spent many years training to be mindful. I raced to the house. My eyes immediately set upon a shadow standing in the doorway. He was surrounded by shattered glass. Upon first inspection, he appeared to be in his late fifties, but he had the body of a thirty-year-old. His fists were grasped around an iron rod.

I stopped; an unusual wave of calmness spread through my body, a complete antithesis to how I felt until then. He began moving toward me. The ferocity in his movements, forceful at first, diminished as he came closer, as though his initial intentions had changed.

The man stopped in front of me and reached for my arm.

"I am sorry... please. I didn't mean to do this," he uttered.

From the corner of my eye, I saw another dark figure emerge from within the house - my sister. She was alive. Relief soared through my veins as she began stumbling in my direction.

I gestured for my sister to come out whilst he was distracted. She trembled with fear, her face twisted into an expression of shock.

"He tried to kill me."

I held onto the feeling of calm within me and met the forceful gaze of the perpetrator whilst she slowly moved out of the house and ran to the car.

"No more damage needs to be done this evening," I murmured, twisting out of his grip. Choosing to express empathy over violence, I looked into his eyes one last time. This time with a look of compassion, before turning around and walking back to the car.

Later, we came to understand he was a failed businessman, the husband of my sister's colleague, and a recent escapee from a mental asylum. He had intentions of killing his wife that night until he crossed paths with my sister.

2

KINDNESS - THE HEAVENLY SPLENDOR

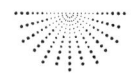

1971,
Southern Sri Lanka.

One glorious morning, I woke to a magical spell. I was ten years old. Gazing out of the window, I saw a majestic view of the small, elegant islands all over the front garden, formed by dewdrops. They were like pebbles on the green grass shining under the sun. I touched them, breaking soft bubbles that spewed chilly air. Inspired by the unique joy, I kept breaking a few more. At that moment, noisy birds on the plum tree grabbed my attention, so I ran to the other end of the garden. Later, I captured that experience in a little poem.

One Kind Bird

Before the dewdrops die,
Sweet little butterfly went searching flowers.
She was stopped by the anxious squirrel.
His eyes were locked into a flock of sparrows,
They were busy eating all the red plums.
Some just played with them.

And one beautiful baby sparrow was all alone,
Talking to a plum,
"My dear red plum,
You are so nice.
I wouldn't trouble you.
The day you become another tree,
I will watch your flowers grow.
And enjoy butterflies and squirrels stopping by to
   add more beauty."

Squirrel whispered to the butterfly,
"Oh darling, she is so charming,
She must be the angel of kindness."

That day, kindness touched my heart. The unique joy struck me. I have known everyone, including birds, butterflies, and squirrels, to understand kindness. It binds us with universal love, instilling happiness and joy. I wanted to explore more about this unusual joy.

Later in life, I discovered the extraordinary character of kindness; it melts our hearts and awakens us from dull contours of concerns to find the common ground of humanity. We feed the hungry, offer refreshment to the thirsty, nurse the sick, and sit with a friend in time of her sorrow. The healing power of kindness will wash away hardships and pain, cultivating zest and happiness.

Kindness earned my highest respect because it didn't seek rewards or acknowledgments. The beauty of kindness lies in its simplicity, authenticity, gentleness, and innocence. Starting the day in the morning, I would share kindness wrapped in pleasant greetings. As the day goes by, kindness dresses up in some other forms of sweet courtesies, helpfulness, and even tolerance. I will uplift the discouraged and share sympathy for those who are burdened and lonely. The splendor of kindness touches me, dissolves my conscious control, and elevates me to a higher level.

As you do, I used to seek happiness in rewards, wealth, and accomplishments. Inside that happiness laid a sense of hollowness that I quelled to fill all the time. Then I found the power of kindness in its extraordinary ability to cement this insidious crack with the feeling of fulfillment. The sublime joy I felt in this process, as I later learned, is the altruistic joy (i.e., *muditha*) - the highest form of happiness one can experience in life according to Buddhist teachings. Acts of kindness result in altruistic joy.

The more I appreciated altruistic joy, the more I would seek opportunities to master the art that would transcend me to practice kindness as a way of life. In the forthcoming sections, you will discover the simple steps (that I have mastered) to develop this art so that you can find the supreme form of happiness - altruistic joy.

3

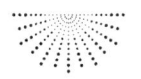

THE BEAST

Kindness is beautiful, but how can its beauty make you happy, successful, and feel complete?

Many know kindness as supporting a charity, or giving money for good causes. Nowadays, these acts of kindness are becoming so popular, even big corporates and celebrities dish them out. The feel-good factor and virtuousness of kindness appeal to us all.

Did you ever imagine kindness can make your life complete with:

- **Happiness**,
- **Prosperity**, and
- **Feeling fulfilled**?

Well, my answer when I began my journey was, "no". Back then, life was unkind. My journey with kindness started because I did not have a choice to get away from depressing poverty. I aimed for education as the way to happiness. That wasn't easy. Yet, I arrived at the peak of educational Everest with a Ph.D. in Biotechnology.

Celebrations kept me happy for a few days. Within weeks, my mind started telling me that prosperity was still missing. Then started another chase - build a business, own a house, gain social status, wealth, and a beautiful family, and so on.

I reached a milestone. Then there was the next one. An insidious creature sitting inside me pointed to another missing piece. I thought this was the norm of life. I kept going. When I fell short, I discovered role models to inspire energy, but they created stress, sadness, inadequacy, and despair. I fell sick. Isn't there a better meaning for life?

Uncovering meaning was like pieces of a jigsaw puzzle. But I have excellent news to share with you: I have found all the pieces of the puzzle!

It took forty years to fix this piece by piece. Though it was long and hard, it was such a joyful journey. The best indicator is that I always feel 'my today is better than yesterday.' At age fifty-eight, I found myself amongst the small minority of individuals on this planet who have seen the path to transcendence.

Transcendence? Yes, and here is the simplest definition of it. Transcendence is rising above the 'self' and reaching beyond the limits of life's everyday experiences. We all are imperfect. That imperfection is an opportunity to improve ourselves and become better. There is joy in humility.

There is no superhuman above you. You are superhuman, but it is still hidden inside you. Kindness can be the panacea to transcend you into that superhuman. You will discover the path in this book.

Here is the most exciting thing: I have defined the formula that compounds the essence of those long lessons into a three-step guide. Yes, only three steps.

I found this three-step formula on the beautiful word - Kindness!

In this book, you will learn this simple three-step guide: Kindness Code. You will discover how to apply kindness to achieve the three most exciting goals in your life:

1. **Sustaining** personal happiness.
2. **Discovering** the path to prosperity.
3. Sustaining **success** and **feeling** fulfilled.

Let's begin this wonderful journey.

4
KINDNESS CODE

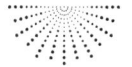

Can we make a magic pill for kindness? One that we can carry in our pockets to grab any time and chew like peppermint to cool the mind and body?

As this is not possible, I have instead discovered a code that can generate kindness.

I have spent years traveling the world, meeting many spiritual teachers, researching science and technology, joining social movements, and entering the world of meditation. After fifty-eight years of experimenting with myself, I discovered the code to generate kindness.

It encapsulates the entire universe of kindness in this code. It is simple yet sophisticated.

Our forefathers, who built our civilization, knew this simple code. They documented it in ancient scripts written in *ola* leaves that were found in ancient temples explaining meditation practices.

I hope that humankind will only use this Kindness Code to develop the mind and experience the power of transcendence, enabling peace and harmony. This will lead to a rediscovery of the utopian dream to banish poverty in favor of affluence and work toward a zero-carbon footprint to save our planet.

Kindness Code is as simple as using a box of matches to ignite a spark to light your candle, and then to light up a million others in your world.

Hold on for one moment; can you imagine that before our ancestors discovered how to harness fire, they used to live in pitch darkness? Since this discovery, civilization has taken giant steps to invent matches, candles, electricity, and all kinds of energy to make our lives brighter, happier, and more efficient.

With that same spirit of discovery, Kindness Code is a formula of simple three steps and two principles:

1. **Ignite**.
2. **Light-up**.
3. **Radiate**.

Step 1: Ignite

Ignite the spark of positive emotion inside you. The joy, gratitude, happiness, satisfaction, and love are a few examples of positive emotions igniting kindness.

Just close your eyes for a moment. Pay attention to your breathing. Think of someone you love most. Can you appreciate that feeling? That is the feeling we need to conjure more to ignite kindness.

Ignite

Radiate

Light-up

Kindness Code

Step 2: Light-up

Light-up is the process through which we stabilize the ignited spark. Remember, a spark is swift. It comes and goes in a fraction of a second. Light-up aims to sustain the life cycle of that spark to a more extended period. It happens within oneself; within you.

Let's recall the analogy of the box of matches. First, we need to create a spark; then, we light a candle. Here, with Kindness Code, the candle is you, and the person lighting the candle is also you.

Step 3: Radiate

As you hold that candle, imagine hundreds of candles around you, and you will light each one with your own. Imagine the beauty of radiating your kindness to light up hundreds of thousands of candles other people hold.

And it all started with one ignite in you. Then came your initiative to light your own candle. Now you're giving light to hundreds and thousands of others. Imagine the brightness and smiles on those faces and happiness in their hearts.

You created that. Celebrate this moment; this is loving-kindness manifesting inside you. Enjoy it. Immerse with the zest and delight of kindness.

In the following sections, you will learn to recreate this powerful feeling. First, it is crucial to recognize that the real impact of kindness comes from applying this three-step code within a framework of two principles;

Principle 1: Be-Kind-to-You-First

The first principle of the Kindness Code is to be kind to yourself first.

Principle 2: Be Kind to Others

To elevate kindness, you must share it with others. Hence, the second principle of the Kindness Code is to radiate kindness to others and to power up the kindness living inside you.

Kindness is magic when we share it with others.

So the theory here is to first ignite kindness within you, then light-up the kindness in you. As a shining light, radiate kindness to the others. This cycle will continue to elevate and empower you and the entire eco-system in which you are living.

In the following chapters, you will learn simple methods to execute these three steps. The goal is to discover and maintain happiness, health, and productivity through simple, practical steps.

However, ignite is the key. It all begins with your ability to discover simple ways and means to ignite. What are those?

IGNITE

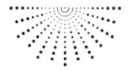

Kindness as **Random Acts**
to
Make your Day **Motivated** and **Happy**.

Ignite

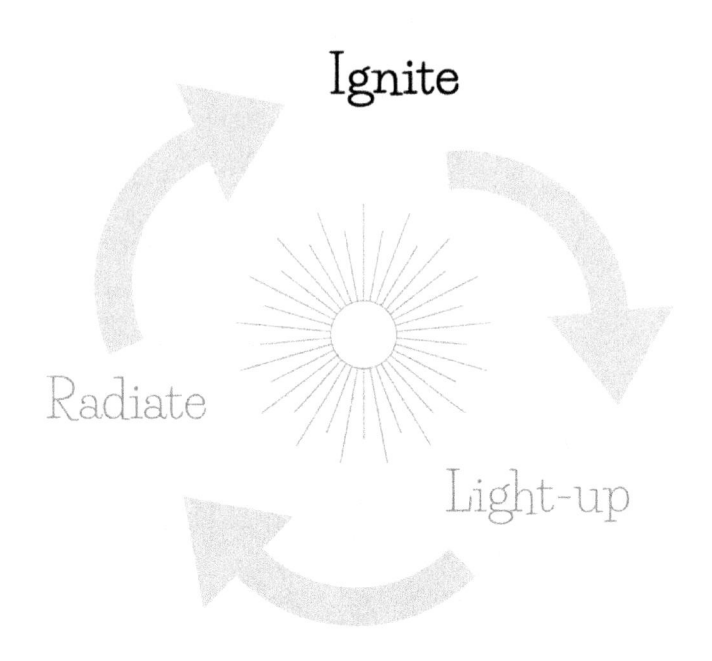

Radiate

Light-up

5
IGNITE KINDNESS WITH POSITIVE IMAGINATION

Daydreaming is fun.

Daydreaming is imagination, enabling us to build visuals in our minds without needing to see them. Can you remember how many things you have imagined without seeing them in actual life? I had traveled around the globe before I even took my first-ever flight. With imagination, we can travel to the past or future, the beach, or even to the moon.

Close your eyes, take a deep breath, and refresh your imagination. The sun, moon, wind, and waves all are there inside your heart. Just pick a few and create a holiday dream. How do you feel? Enjoy happiness, making no carbon footprint.

Daydreams generate positive emotions. Writing about the power of positive thinking, Johns Hopkins Medicine explains, "The mechanism for the connection between health and positivity remains murky. But researchers suspect that people who are more positive may be better protected against stress. Another possibility is that hope and positivity help people make better health and life decisions and focus more on long-term goals."

Steadfast in belief, envision your daydreams vividly; the prescription for daydreaming. Visualization is more than mere intention. Create a complete visual image of the desired outcome. Let's say you dream of taking part in a marathon. Visualize the location, other athletes around you, and their colorful gear, then find your spot and get ready for the starting whistle. The motivation, excitement, and poise made by this exercise ignite kindness. Try the following steps as a guide to experimenting with positive imagination.

- Find a quiet, comfortable place, and sit and close your eyes.
- Take a deep breath. Imagine you are inhaling positive energy and exhaling negative energy.
- Start visualizing the things you wish to have. Your visualization will be through your mind's eye. Visualize them in as much detail as possible, as if they are already present. Enjoy the feeling.
- Once you are fully immersed through this positive imagination, pay attention to the surroundings.
- Gently open your eyes. Now reflect on how you felt.

In my early stages, I focused on inherently confident simple dreams; for example, receiving birthday gifts or having a Christmas celebration were simple to visualize. They boosted my emotions at any time and helped ignite kindness.

Daydreaming comes naturally for many. Yet, for some, it is difficult. Painful memories of unfortunate events in their history can become a barrier; thus, I have explored other optional routes to ignite kindness, which I will explain next.

6
MOTHER NATURE IS HEAVENLY

Nature is an excellent source in which to ignite kindness; it holds many secrets. I once met a lady who gave me a hint so that I could discover another route to ignite.

"Romance is not my favorite cup of tea." Her free-spirited words were soft and touching. This stranger's entertaining stories grabbed my attention at a coffee shop before I caught my train at London-Victoria station.

"I find love in a falling leaf. How beautiful it is. The green color, the veins, the oval shaped body ending with a tip. That tip is so powerful. When I see a tiny dewdrop hanging onto that tiny tip, I feel like a baby hanging onto the mother. The entire flow of energy lies at that tip. I can't help but touch it. That transforms my mood."

She found love in nature. Nature has deep secrets to offer love. Look at the flowers, birds, rivers, golden beaches, and sunshine - they are all incredible sources of positive energy.

They have the power to generate positive emotions in our hearts and minds. They ignite kindness.

Let me explain how I decoded the hidden art that lady mastered to tap into nature:

1. She was careful to choose things that make her feel better.
2. She observed them in greater detail.
3. She was grateful for the love and happiness they generated in her.

It was a matter of:

- **Choosing,**
- **Appreciation**, and
- **Gratification.**

So, the lesson here is to choose the things in nature that motivate you to feel positive and happy, then appreciate them to enhance those positive emotions. By being grateful, you develop those positive emotions further, which allows you to use nature to ignite kindness.

7

THE RIVER FLOWS WITH HAPPINESS

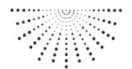

My favorite childhood retreat was visiting my grandparents. With my two sisters, we used to count the days down to school holidays, where we would embark on the long bus journey to the glorious escape.

Visits to the crowded central bus station in polluted Colombo city were not pleasant. My eager eyes awaited the escape; yet, it was slow. The bus driver struggled to negotiate through unruly traffic. An hour into the journey, the bus sped up, and the landscape changed, replacing the concrete buildings with golden beaches and blue sea waves. The excitement in my sister's eyes surged as we drew closer to the beautiful destination, Galle - a well-known tourist attraction in Sri Lanka.

Yet, the splendor of the rural cottage in which my grandparents lived was not on the seafront; it was the lovely river swirling below the small hill. The moment we entered their home, I would sprint to my favorite hilltop lookout. Scenic views of the flowing water fondling the banks of wildflower meadows, breaking sunbeams over the blue water, made it majestic.

We'd cuddle in bed, listening to grandpa read us stories. Still, my mind would sneak into the awaiting anticipation of the morning ritual.

We'd spend hours playing in the river every morning. Calm and quiet water flow; petals of a flower, one behind the other; floating dragonflies, often dancing over a drifting branch of a dead tree. We would count the blue pebbles buried in golden sand in the shallow riverbed.

The pebbles, sand, petals, dragonflies, and water all form an eco-system that depends on each other. They love and care. Immersing with the river, we all join that stream of love to celebrate that love feast.

Rivers are rich reservoirs of nature's beauty secrets. They provide immense opportunities to ignite positive emotions, opening the gateway to kindness.

8

CHERRY BLOSSOMS AND SMILES

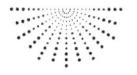

Spring 1988, Japan.

"It looks simple. At least I can handle this without chopsticks." My thoughts were abrupt as it tired me to study the menu. Besides, I was a novice stepping into a new life in a foreign country, just after forty-eight hours from landing.

After about ten minutes, the waiter appeared with a tray. On top was a thinly sliced full bowl of cabbage, nothing else. I started eating the tasteless cabbage, hiding my disappointment. The next minute, this caring waiter brought me a small black bottle of soy sauce. My dispirited mind further struggled in the presence of the thoughtful, over-polite simple man.

The cultural shock was overbearing. Illiteracy of the Japanese language rattled my confidence; I felt like a lonely child on many occasions - finding the way to the train station, operating an automated ticket machine, even standing in line at a supermarket.

Outpouring compassion from every Japanese person replaced my anxiety with comfort. Goto-san, the Japanese tutor, was my savior. We had one thing in common - he wanted to learn English, and I wanted to learn Japanese.

"Konnichiwa."

Goto-san's greeting astonished me. I didn't expect him at my student dormitory that day. *"Oh dear, I forgot to greet."* I was ashamed, but Goto-san made me comfortable as he continued the conversation.

"We are planning to visit *Hanami*." He paused for a moment and looked at his English dictionary to check his accuracy of the translation. Then he made a shy laugh, looking sideways before starting the next sentence. "*Hana* means flowers... and, and... *Hana-mi* is seeing flowers." He worked hard to educate me before another international student jumped in to fill the gap.

"Harsha, that is the Sakura festival - the most exciting festival in the spring; don't miss it!"

We visited Ueno Park, the famous site for the Sakura festival in Tokyo. Cherry blossoms brought exceptional comfort to my troubled mind. Happy campers threw parties under cherry trees, everyone brought barbecues, beer, and laughter. These cherry blossoms had brought Heaven to Earth.

I saw a drunken lad having fun with flower petals that had fallen into his beer glass. He threw his fingers in deep to pick the petals out and put them into his mouth, *"Oishie... dayo."*

His girlfriend raised her glass, too, *"Honthoniee!"*

Oishie means 'tasty.' That was among the first few Japanese words I learned.

Among thousands of onlookers, one older woman took my attention. She was short and wore a puffy blue top concealing her ailing pale body. Her noticeable breathing tubes were connected to an oxygen cylinder lying in the cart she pushed. She was a sufferer; yet, her push was vigorous.

Moving aside, I kept observing her eager eyes, wandering between cherry blossoms and busy joyful campers. They stopped for a moment at the young drunken couple whom I saw before. A pleasant smile appeared on her face as she beheld the funny dance the petal-eating boy was now doing under a cherry tree. Then she moved her cart forward into the crowd.

She knew the art of igniting kindness out of this Sakura festival, where dancing blossoms spread positive energy into every mind.

9

HILLS IN THE MIST INFUSES POSITIVE VIBES

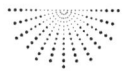

Ethiopia, 2014.

I was on a business trip to meet some local communities in a region of Mekelle, one of the country's beauty spots.

After a brief flight from Addis Ababa, it was amusing to see a driver holding my name upside down. His wandering eyes turned into a broad smile when I signaled him; the stranger he waited to pick up was me.

The panorama of mountains in the distance would stop anyone stepping out of the small terminal building. A few miles into the trip, we arrived at the heart of it. The view of the majestic mountain standing like a giant rising from the landscape was intimidating.

'Wow, this is huge.' I could not hold my excitement. The driver was busy steering the Jeep through the steep winding road. His head moved as he drove over tricky curves.

The consistent climb took us from one hill to another. One summit captured my attention; it was breathtaking. Before I finished appreciating it, another summit appeared. Peeping through the window, moving back and forth to enjoy full astonishment of the view, I felt like a child again.

I turned to the driver, "Do you need a break?"

It took a while for him to understand my words, even with the help of my sign language.

He nodded his head, adding a smile to his confused face, saying, "No, I am fine; let's carry on." By now, we were both drained after five long hours of driving; I was yearning for some fresh Ethiopian coffee from a local cafe, but there was none to be found.

With legs crippled, and pelvic area feeling like molded rods, I felt as though I were a tortured animal. My dizzy mind dreamed of rest. The hotel room was the only aspiration to bring life back.

We arrived and settled into the room. I took a shower and sank into a comfortable chair next to the window. The sparkling beauty of the hilltops in the distance captured my eyes. They eased my mental muscles. In stark contrast to the grumpy, heavy feeling I had a while ago, I was now vibrant. I turned on the computer to use Skype.

"Hey, how are you? It was a glorious trip. I am in a beautiful room watching hilltops in the distance!"

It was such a long day. The hills ignited my kindness to overcome the travel fatigue.

10

BEACH: ESCORTING WAVES OF HOPES

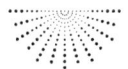

Oh, another sigh!

His sighs kept growing, and now they sounded high-pitched to disturb my half-asleep mind. Still, eyes closed, I moved to his side. "Come on... there's no point worrying, you'll know by tomorrow. You will be fine."

"Yes, I know... but... but... I don't know how to tell mom if I fail. She's bragging about me to all the neighbors. You know what she's like, don't you?" His whining prompted me to open my eyes.

"Hm," I sighed looking toward the ceiling.

"Well, you always did better than me. I am sure the results will be great." I continued comforting him, though deep inside, I had a stronger feeling that I would have done better this time.

The next morning, we got the exam results, and there was a piece of delightful news: my friend exceeded his expectations. He joined the cheering crowd in the noisy dormitory, and I found the exit door, all alone.

"Damn-it." I kicked an empty Coca Cola can on the pavement; it made an eerie noise over the empty alley. A bus slowed down, ready to disembark its passengers in the distance. I sprinted onto the crowded bus to run away from the university environment, where everyone spoke only about exam results.

"This can't be correct. I can appeal anyway," I told my mind to silence its chatter.

When the bus approached the seaside, my instincts guided me to a quiet corner. I found a rock on the beach on which to rest my back. It was my familiar rock that I used to call my 'dream rock.' Today, it was not helpful. I stood and walked to the water.

The breaking waves at a distance made a gigantic blasting sound in my eardrums; then they broke into the frothy-beautiful chain of baby waves in front of my eyes. Mother nature held my hand and took me into her world of love and kindness.

I kept walking. Every time my feet sank into the sand, the somber feeling diminished little by little. I could feel sizeable chunks of despair disappear at once, and gentle warmth began to replace the empty pockets.

Over five miles into the walk, I found my inner child coming alive with an urge to build a sandcastle again. I rediscovered my strengths and confidence to return to meet my friends, most of whom were toasting their success.

The beach is one of the beautiful things that make our planet Earth Heaven. We love it. We never feel tired sitting there, walking over wet-golden sand, building sandcastles, and sketching designs on the sand. A great wonder to ignite kindness.

11

SUNSHINE SPARKS HAPPINESS

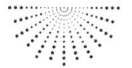

I knew she was in a bit of a struggle by the way she knocked on the door. My daughter stepped in and tiptoed over the white carpet as if she were walking over a fragile glass pane.

"I don't know what to do." Her whisper was weak. "I couldn't sleep at all. It's all coming to my head like broken pieces, but I don't get how to put them together… something is missing." She paused for a moment. "It's in a cloud over there, but I can't get it… ya, see?" She had been working on this artwork for her final-year project for over a month.

"I will submit the completed design before five p.m. today." She sounded strained and anxious.

The looming deadline was only hours away. Her desperation made me speechless. I walked a few steps up and down, staring at the floor, still silent. A sunbeam fell through the window, sparking hope to help her out.

"Let's go for a walk." I led her out the door as she dragged her feet. "Oh, come on, let's get some fresh air. It is a gorgeous morning," I said.

The chirpy birds uplifted my tone, allowing me to push her to follow my footsteps toward the apple orchard. The mild chill in the air softened the heaviness in my mind. I felt they would soften her nervousness, too. But the thin bubble of my self-confidence was about to rupture. Any moment, she might ask to turn around.

I stopped at an apple tree. "Look at this beautiful flower smiling at you. She must have endured the dark, chilly night. See those dewdrops; they must be hurting. But this flower is finding her way out to enjoy the sunshine. She is working hard to deliver a baby apple."

Puzzled by her silence, I looked at my daughter. Her eyes stayed locked onto those flowers. Sunshine glowed over her face, softening her facial muscles.

"Take a deep breath, darling." I started guiding her into silent meditation. Sunshine brought inspiration and vibrancy from nowhere.

"Okay... I've got to go now." Her characteristic cocky tone reminded me of her swagger as it returned. She beamed, inspired to infuse newly found creative energy into her design work. A few hours later, I saw her heading back to university with the drawing carrier case tucked into her shoulder.

"thanx. all done. lve u." The text message was cute.

Catching a few rays of sunlight during the day can make a world of difference. Many scientists have established bright sunny days to boost mood. After long, dreary days of chilly winter, we all get excited with the spring sunshine; even birds migrate to tropical regions to seek sunlight. Trees find new vigor, and flowers turn to fruits. Sunshine is a natural booster to ignite kindness in our human mind.

12
WILDFLOWER MEADOWS ARE TENDERING

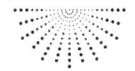

Why did it happen? Why didn't I tell the police the actual story? At least I could have recovered the passport, which could have saved my travel plan!

Yesterday, someone stole my laptop bag from right under my seat. The incident happened as I attended an intense business meeting in a coffee shop at Paddington Station. I lost my passport and laptop. Many project files developed over the past years had gone missing along with the laptop. Extensive business travel to ten countries was impending starting the following week. Travel visas and hotel bookings were not conceivable without the passport.

I approached a policeman to report the incident. His eyes scanned me from tip to toe before fixing into mine. Then, he tuned in to my explanation. "We get many complaints about losing laptops every day. London Paddington is a bustling station, sir." His calm voice settled me.

After an abrupt pause looking thoughtfully downward, he raised his head again. "Would you have any suspects in mind?"

I had a clue; the Eastern European waiter looked suspicious as he made eye contact during many rounds of coffee-serves to feed our intense conversations. But without having concrete evidence, I chose not to complain about the poor guy.

It took some time to find words to explain the full story to my wife, after returning home with a baffled and desolate mind. "Take a rest. Let time heal your mind." I complied with her thoughtful advice.

The next morning, I woke with a fresh mind as usual; yet, it didn't take long for those killer memories to torment my culpable mind. I was despondent and falling prey to the cascading sorrow.

Before those emotions buried me deep in paralysis, I gulped down some coffee and started walking toward the meadows. The entry path covered by bushes was narrow and dark. I sped up my dragging feet to counter the creeping vulnerability. Soon, a bright vista of grasslands appeared through the corridor of bushes. That infused some vigor.

The bridge crossing through the river was lonely but welcomed me to the heartland of tranquility; the rhythmic sound of flowing water, sudden flaps of a goose taking off, and an appealing call by a lonely breeding bird nearby.

The wind connected me with silent meadow voices. An occasional crack of a dead leaf under my shoe broke that silence to remind me I was in a walking meditation.

I stopped to cherish the artful swim of a duck crossing the breadth of the lake; the water trail left by her journey still recovering. That sight dressed my emotional wounds.

I heard a spontaneous whisper, "Why bother? Here is Heaven. Enjoy the gift!"

The wind, smell, warmth, and peace ignited positive energy. I walked back home and started planning how to control further damages, including resetting passwords and informing banks. Finally, I told my clients about potential changes to the travel plans. Wildflower meadows ignited kindness in me.

13

PUPPY IS DANCING

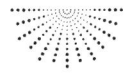

I returned home after a long, hard day. As I grew closer, my heartbeat rose. Excitement exploded the moment I opened the door and saw her appear from nowhere; she began her dance, tail wagging with a lovely low-pitched moan.

"Welcome home," that's what she told me before leading me to the kitchen.

"How was your day? Did you sleep all day, cheeky?" I continued my conversation as she took me to her doggy pot to show me she had cleared everything. I cuddled her and started our discussion.

Dogs are friends; I can talk about anything with her. She listens. I was sure she could understand every bit of my emotions then, because she responded to every emotion more than my friends did.

The day my sister wrote a letter saying my ninety-year-old grandma was ill, I struggled. I changed my plans to visit the cinema with friends, as I wanted to be alone. Then I laid on the couch. My puppy sat down near me, and I started talking. She fixed her shining eyes and settled down to hear more. I told her many childhood stories about our grandma; we both cried.

Many of us share our secrets with the dog because they listen so well and never dispute our intentions. Then again, they never spill the beans.

Someone said all dogs are natural comedians. They make fun, and their dynamism energizes us and spreads joy wherever they go, from morning walks to evening drives into town. She would sit in the back seat and enjoy the breeze through the window as I drove the car around.

Dogs never hold grudges against our mistakes. And they always welcome a cuddle and make us feel better. Their healing and soothing ability are magical. I am sure they love us just as much as we love them.

With these exceptional qualities, dogs are a brilliant companion in igniting our kindness; not only dogs but also any pet would do that for you. They can ignite kindness in us anywhere at any time. The art is how we appreciate that quality. The positive energy they ignite in our minds then master the skill to 'be-with-it.' The more we learn this art, the more you may find how easy it is to ignite kindness at will.

If you are not a natural pet lover, this would not be the best method. I trust the next technique may be helpful for you to ignite kindness.

14
POSITIVE QUOTES TO IGNITE KINDNESS

One morning, a doctor I know well had to decide how to inform Albert, her patient, that he had cancer. After a lengthy discussion, she told Albert it was unlikely he would live to see his next birthday, which was due in a few months. The following day, the doctor received a beautiful card;

Dear doctor,

When it rains, I look for the rainbow. When it is dark, I look for stars.

- Albert.

It was signed with a smiling face and a big thank you. And he has lived many years more than the doctor predicted.

A good quote can make a monumental difference to ignite positive energy. On a dull day, I would search Google for an appropriate quote to inspire me. I would go through a few quotes to find the right motivation. It always works.

Positive quotes are a brilliant source to ignite kindness. Some of which include:

> "My religion is kindness. It is very simple."
>
> — HIS HOLINESS DALAI LAMA.

> "Kindness is the language which the deaf can hear, and the blind can see."
>
> — MARK TWAIN.

> "Kindness is like snow. It beautifies everything it covers."
>
> — KAHLIL GIBRAN.

> "Carry out a random act of kindness, with no expectation of reward, safe in the knowledge that someone might do the same for you one day."
>
> — PRINCESS DIANA.

> "Kindness makes you the most beautiful person in the world, no matter what you look like."
>
> — ANONYMOUS.

Igniting kindness is as simple as effectively tapping into these resources, such as nature, and positive quotes and imagination. I am sure you may discover a few more easy tricks in which to ignite kindness.

The irony, however, is that ignite alone cannot sustain kindness. Positive emotions, such as happiness, love, and inspiration, are so fragile. They often disappear in a second, which is why we need the second step of Kindness Code: light-up!

15

CHEMISTRY

1989, Tokyo, Japan.

Occupied with plant tissues, it confined my entire day to the tissue culture laboratory. The powerful artificial lights illuminated the air-conditioned room for twenty-four hours. The roar of the ventilator often disrupted the smooth music from my Sony speaker system. In this energetic room, days passed by without seeing the sunlight. The tender plants grown inside the test tubes were my children. Often, I used to talk to them. That day, just before midnight, I suddenly remembered that the following day would be the birthday of the most beloved person in my life: Ana.

I rushed to my notebook and opened a new blank page.

My darling,
They say,
A rose by any other name is still a rose.
But this one is different,
Grown inside a test tube,
Infused with a lot of love.
Treated by a kind-hearted,
Sitting inside a laboratory, all alone.
- Happy birthday, my love!

This poem, written on the birthday card, explains another remarkable phenomenon: the chemicals behind the spirit of love and kindness.

Our entire planet is a blend of chemicals. Every plant, insect, and animal comprises of chemical compounds. If we color-coded all those compounds, it would create a beautiful infographic. Scientists have organized this infographic into the 'Periodic table' - the one many of us learn in school. They reduce the entire planet to one hundred and eighteen elements.

These elements are organized into unique formations, shapes, beings, and events. When our sensory organs, such as eyes, ears, and tongue, interact with such formations, they produce a sensation. Our brain then gives a name to that sensory experience; apples and oranges, butterflies and bees, sweet and bitter, or songs and words.

There is another striking aspect of these sensory experiences; they are conveyed between different parts of the body, again by chemical compounds. Scientists call them hormones.

For us to feel love, we need the love hormone, oxytocin, which is released from our pituitary gland and distributed to other tissues and organs. We love that sensation called 'love.' In the same vein, scientists like to attribute the 'feel-good' feeling of kindness to four essential hormones: serotonin, oxytocin, dopamine, and endorphins.

This understanding of chemicals and hormones, particularly the way they affect our kindness, is useful for the skillful execution of the Kindness Code.

In our analogy of a box of matches to generate fire, our sensory organs are the 'matches,' and outside formations, such as shapes, beings, and events, are the 'surfaces.' When these 'matches' scratch these 'surfaces,' ignite occurs, causing flickers of emotions.

As explained previously, nature inspires us, sunshine brings energy, and flowers inspire love and motivation. How do we master this art of igniting kindness to make every move an artful stroke of kindness during our busy lives?

We need to build routines and habits to keep us motivated. If you commute daily to work, think about cultivating a few little habits of reading positive news, listening to calm music, or helping someone in need. How about routines such as donating a coffee to a stranger every Monday morning, or making Friday a vegan day? These will help spark positive energy at regular intervals during the day and week.

Then again, what happens when boredom takes control as the sun sets? When rain ruins your evening party? What if the electricity goes off just before meeting your crucial deadline? And even worse, when the doctor discloses, in carefully chosen words, that you have cancer? Oh!

Suddenly, the wind is blowing; a storm is brewing. The candle is about to lose its fire!

We humans can't live alone; we need a healthy support system. We often refer to this support system as "relationships." I will show you how kindness plays a crucial role in this territory, and how to keep your candle burning - even during a brutal storm.

LIGHT-UP

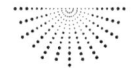

Kindness as a **Thought Process**
to
Elevate,
Immerse in **Love**, and
Achieve **Prosperity**.

Ignite

Radiate

Light-up

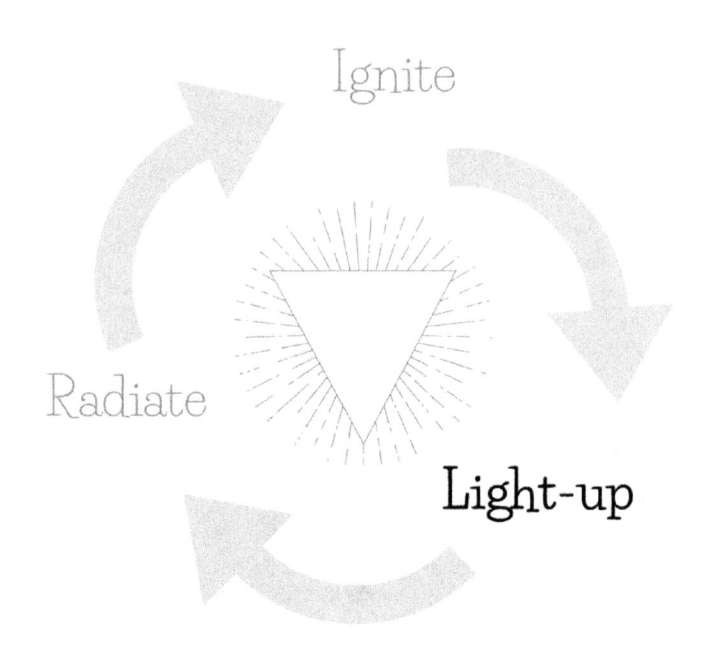

16

BE-KIND-TO-YOU-FIRST

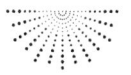

We are gifted to be alive in this beautiful modern world. As accomplished individuals, we want to be free and independent; yet, as biological creatures, we are connected to a fabric of interdependence by design. We can't live in this world without the support of family, friends, or social relationships in that nexus of interdependence.

- We need someone to share our happiness and hugs, attend to specific needs, keep secrets, and escalate our triumphs to new heights.
- We need someone to listen to our grievances, tolerate our anger, or sit next to us silently with a big open heart to fill our loneliness.
- We need suppliers of daily requirements such as food, water, medicines, and shelter.

In this web of relationships, there is a 'me,' and there is a 'them.' We trade kindness as beautiful gift wrapping. We all feel bad if someone cannot use this wrapping; then we call it being unkind!

"Should I be kind to them first? Or should I be kind to myself first?"

It is not uncommon to have that question, and perhaps more.

"Is it morally appropriate to be kind to myself first?"

"Where is the altruism?"

Every time I would take a flight, I used to enjoy the flight attendants' artful maneuvers just before takeoff. When they announced, 'in an unlikely event of a flight emergency, please attend to yourself first before attending to your child,' I struggled and questioned its morality. Later, I would understand the logic in research studies related to human behavior.

In our hearts, we wish to stay on our moral high ground. We admire kindness; it drives our urgency to radiate kindness to others. Yet, ironically, our personal capacity falls short. This is because nature has programmed us to be self-centered in our behavior, creating a kindness conundrum - lack of clarity in which to judge the prioritization between 'me' or 'them.'

As human beings, we need to ensure physical survival first. Well-known Maslow's Hierarchy of Needs emphasizes that one must satisfy basic needs before attending to psychological and social ones.

Noble Eightfold Path is a core teaching that describes the code of conduct for Buddhist practitioners. Self-restraint is a fundamental practice introduced in those teachings. In monastery retreats, Buddhist monks teach meditation techniques for the layman in training body and mind to develop such fundamentals. They educate to find the clarity in judgment and to look after personal health and wellbeing before attending to others.

It is perfectly appropriate for one to look after their own health and wellbeing before attending to others. It does not make altruism second-rated. We will talk more on that aspect later.

With this in mind, the Kindness Code's light-up phase is where we deliberately aim to be kind to yourself first! Look at the candle in your hand, grip it, and make the flame stable and robust. This perspective illustrates **Principle #1** of the Kindness Code: **Be-Kind-to-You-First**.

This component of the Kindness Code aims to direct kindness toward you by building and nurturing appropriate relationships and having those relationships support your positive emotions.

17

EXPRESS YOUR LOVE (BETTER)

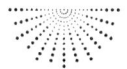

The flight was about to pushback to start a twelve-hour journey. I stood up, unfastening the seat belt. The air hostess in business-class gaped at me, stopping her pre-flight preparations before the take-off maneuver. "Sorry... I just need to... my family are sitting in economy... i'll be right back," I briskly said before she spoke.

Striding through the catering cabin, I noticed another hostess turning to call at me, "Excuse me, sir. We are about to take off."

I waved at her, peeping through the curtains to the right side, economy class front row.

My wife, sitting in the center, seized her seatbelt fastening and stared open-mouthed. "You alright?"

I just stopped for a moment, surveying our two daughters sitting on either side. The elder seated at the aisle side, still fixated on a book, while the other enjoyed the outside view at the window. My wife kept rolling her eyes.

I sneaked a moment of privacy, looking into my wife's curious eyes.

"*Dido!*" I whispered, triggering an instantaneous shy smile exchanged between my wife and me. I saw my elder daughter taking her eyes off the book, looking curiously at me as I turned to retreat.

Before another crew member rambled her discontent, I became apologetic. "Sorrrry… I am returning to my seat."

Settling down in my seat, I felt some comfort. "Now, I am ready to enjoy business class treatment." Until then, I felt guilty sitting in business all alone, with my family in economy.

When we chose advanced booking, we planned to be on two different flights. Though we headed to the same destination, the first part of the trip was for my business work. Yet, a change in circumstances put us all on the same flight.

Now, I felt guilty about enjoying the business class treatments of a twelve-hour-long flight all alone. And, although my wife and children expressed their understanding, I felt terrible.

The next day, at the Airbnb, we sat for breakfast when my daughters started smiling at each other.

"Guess what, ha…. haa…. we finally figured out all about your *dido!*" My second daughter started explaining the decoding of the secret code my wife and I had had for over thirty years.

"Why don't you just say, 'I love you?'" My elder daughter joined the conversation while both Ana and myself kept silent. We both smiled, yet we did not speak up.

About thirty years ago, we discovered the word *dido* while watching a movie at the cinema. The loving couple in that movie used the word '*dido*' instead of 'I love you' to express love between each other. That was an excellent discovery for us both, living in Eastern culture in Sri Lanka. Unlike in the West, in our cultures, expressing love in public was not universal.

We both maintained it as a secret practice. Even back in the UK, we still could not come out of that cultural upbringing. Hence, on various occasions, *dido* was our word of expression, in front of children, which they could not decode.

Since that day, somehow, we had lost the secret feeling of that word. But we both know the substantial power of the word to spark our feelings and bond our relationship over thirty years. We are helping light-up kindness.

18

IT IS OKAY TO BE VULNERABLE

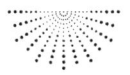

We settled down on a bench overlooking the vast green field. At the end of the ten-day meditation retreat, our minds were still waking up from the serenity.

Stefano was an Italian novelist; we met at a meditation retreat. When I explained to him about light-up kindness, he shared his story on vulnerability.

"It was nineteen ninety-four, and we were living in Florence," Stefano began. "My wife was four months pregnant with our first son. I was in the middle of writing my second book, *Exposed*."

"Catalina, the protagonist, was an inspirational woman. But while developing this character, I found some roots in my ex-girlfriend. By chance, within weeks we happened to meet at a party, and she agreed to sit with me for some interviews. Some questions were intimate, surrounding her sex life. At times, as a newly married husband, I felt moral boundaries were being tested."

"Oh, trust me, I could hold my guard." He paused with a sigh. "I am a good husband." He looked at me in affirmation.

"One day, my sister called me saying, my wife had confided in her and had explained that she was unhappy in our relationship and was going to take a break. She was going to move back in with her parents. This was alarming news; it was extraordinary for her to reveal that, when I live with my wife twenty-four hours a day, as I work from home, cook, talk, and share all my stories. I help her out every day at keeping the house. What else could I possibly give her? I was confused and angry."

Listening to Stefano, I remembered Leon F. Sheltzer, a clinical psychologist and author, who blogs in *Psychology Today*. "The moment someone criticizes you, you feel vulnerable; your knee-jerk reaction is to do everything possible to escape it. It is an inherent aspect of our survival instincts. With courage, we can surpass this impulsive foolhardiness to discover a rational sense." That is what Stefano explained next.

"Later, I visited my sister to get a more detailed perspective. Those conversations revealed how my busy writer's mind might have blindfolded the caring husband duties to a wife facing pregnancy complications. Even worse, I had come to rebuke her for suspicious actions, yet she did not once complain about my ex-girlfriends involvement with my book. I felt guilty, confused, and vulnerable, with a looming danger to our marriage life."

"I felt worried, what if she had seen my interview manuscripts?" His head was down, upper body bent forward, looking at me again.

"I did not find a way to discuss the matter, and I suspended interviews with my ex-girlfriend."

He choked, "Basically… I had to stop developing Catalina."

"Then, this is the most important part, Harsha!" There was a sudden change to his tone. "I planned a trip to her parents over the weekend, which was overdue for months. I ordered a book in my wife's name and sent it to her parent's address — a book titled *Dare to Lead; Brave Work, Tough Conversations, Whole Hearts* by Brene Brown."

"You might have read about Brene Brown. She is so inspirational." I took special note to read her book later.

"The day we arrived at her parents," Stefano continued. "I surprised her when she saw the book in the post. She was even more excited to see the letter enclosed inside the book with a three-day holiday package."

"A-ha. That was a magic move," I could not help applauding his creativity.

"Yes, it was. The next day, I saw her reading the book. I was surprised when she pointed out a quote written in it."

Brene Brown writes, in her book, "Vulnerability is not winning or losing; it's having the courage to show up and be seen when we have no control over the outcome. Vulnerability is not weakness; it's our greatest measure of courage."

"All alone in the holiday bungalow, we started the first day just walking around the farm. She got tired, so we returned halfway, and I spent the afternoon preparing a special lasagna that night. She loved that I felt so happy."

"The next day, I invited her to listen to my story's plot. I showed her some scenes that explained the characters involved in the book. That evening, she started giving me more ideas on Catalina - some fine details she found that I had missed in the character's plot. They were super good insights."

"By the third day, I showed her a dramatic scene involving vulgarity of the Catalina character. It was risky; I thought she might reject or perhaps get angry. Yet, can you believe she said she liked that scene and started giving me more insights? Unbelievable!" His voice was full of energy.

"The trust and confidence in her words were most appealing to me. I got a rush of blood to expand the plot's unwritten scenes. Wow, that creative spark was exceptional."

"The creative partnership that came through her was so amazing, yet…" Stefano paused again, "probably the most relieving part was her empathy and reassurance of love and care."

Vulnerability, cheating, and ineffective communication were widely reported among the top ten key reasons contributing to relationships breaking down in the UK. Stefano was an outstanding example in light-up kindness to secure relationships, turning vulnerability into a strength.

Vulnerability is an asset if we learn the art of using it as a strength.

19
THE WORST TRUTH IS BETTER THAN THE SWEETEST LIE

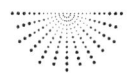

The truth is in us, our minds and lives, and the nature surrounding us. Our living manifests the reality of our interdependent existence with nature.

"The power of truth never declines," quoted by the Dalai Lama, an enduring personality of truthfulness and honesty. Living in exile in India, he is the spiritual leader for the Tibetan people, giving those who suffer under the brutal oppression by Chinese authorities a voice.

As the leader of the Tibetan community, he chose compassion and honesty amidst oppression and negative propaganda.

Surrounded by hardships, he continues to live life with truth, guiding the masses to radiate compassion. Every human being in the world reveres him for this extraordinary quality.

Yet, in our day-to-day life, we take the comfort of bending the truth. New terms such as paltering and white lies provide some light into inventive ways of lying, which often many of us erroneously perceive as ethically accepted. Paltering, a term known among psychologists, means using truthful facts to deceive someone; it helps to project you as a trustworthy person while still being a liar.

In BBC Future's article titled *The devious art of lying by telling the truth*, Melissa Hogenboom writes, "A classic example might be if your mum asks if you've finished your homework and you respond 'I've written an essay on Tennessee Williams for my English class.' It may be true, but it doesn't answer whether you had done your homework. You could have written that essay long ago, and you have misled your poor mother with a truthful statement. You might not have even started your homework yet."

White lies refer to the use of pure lies, such as 'you are beautiful' to satisfy someone to achieve your hidden goals, such as asking a favor. In my early days, I used to say, "I really love that book you gave me," though I didn't even open a page. I intended to avoid hurting the other party who gave me the gift. Yet later, I found an alternative. Instead, I would say, "I am sorry I couldn't read it yet, but I honestly appreciate your intention." There is a big difference between telling the truth versus the use of truthful information to mislead.

In the spirit of kindness, we work hard to avoid self-cheating. In the book *The Art of Happiness*, the Dalai Lama explains, "The more honest you are, the less fear you will have because there's no anxiety about being exposed or revealed to others."

A wise man once said, "I always tell the truth because it is the easiest thing to remember."

We waste energy and time when we avoid telling the truth. When you are honest, you don't have to maintain an artificial guard, testing and censoring what you explain to others. Letting go of secrets is liberating; it empowers you. Be kind to be truthful. That is light-up.

20

KINDNESS WITHOUT CONFRONTING EGO

Alms round is a unique tradition in the Buddhist monastic life. One monk I used to know endeavored to maintain this daily ritual. Come rain or shine, he never broke it. Walking miles through the mountainous tropical forest of Central Sri Lanka, he reached out to the village community for alms. Though villagers were willing to bring food to the monk at his jungle monastery, he hardly ever allowed it.

One day, I inquired about his reasoning behind this ritual.

"We monks preach sermons to the village community who visit the monastery in the evenings. There, we are revered teachers, and they are the students. Then the next morning, we perform in the alms round begging for food. We stay in front of their doorsteps. Now, they are the donors to feed our empty stomachs."

"Both monks and lay communities maintain humbleness through this practice. It is such a powerful technique introduced in the Buddhist tradition to tame the complex ego."

The monk continued, "Not everyone is equally devoted when I go alms round into new communities. There are situations; they close the door in front of me."

He looked around before starting his next story, "One day, a psychotic man directed an angry dog at me during my alms round. He pulled my robe to pieces." The monk paused for a moment and looked down, "I felt tears. Then, my meditative mind reminded me: look at those tears, now understand your ego."

Years later, this monk arrived at a monastery in the UK. He continued his walks in close-by towns and cities during the summer. One morning, a middle-aged woman approached him as he stood quietly for someone to offer alms. Not being familiar with the Buddhist tradition, she asked many questions. And the last was a tough one.

"You are young and strong. Do you think it is fair to beg from older people like me, who still work hard to earn a living?"

After a long pause, the monk broke his silence. "I have become a monk to understand life's meaning. One discipline I have to adopt in my tradition is not using money. And everything I learn I share with others. I offer them this for free. We call it *dana* sharing."

The lady went to a nearby supermarket and brought him a cheese and onion sandwich and an apple juice. The following week, the same lady arrived at the monastery to learn more about Buddhism.

In the affair of kindness, the ego-complex poses barriers. Light-up is a process where we learn the skills to discipline our ego, and often the outcomes are empowering.

21

MANAGING CONFLICTS IN RELATIONSHIPS

We love birthdays and weddings; we all join the love and happiness shared by friends and families. When we pass exams, we share that joy with them and vice versa. That is the natural part.

What about conflict, complaints, and blame games? We often face awkward moments in our dealings with friends, families, and others. How do we light-up kindness in such difficult situations?

My closest friends used to influence my feelings. One day, I noticed my best friend had fallen into a grim mood. Yet, the moment I approached him asking, "How can I help you?" he burst into anger, blaming me for something I could not relate to at all.

That incident put me into an emotional prison for days. The irony was that my other friends navigated through his emotions without falling into any conflict.

"Why did I become the victim for undue blame?"

"Am I too soft? Then how can I be tough?"

The following is an action sequence we can introduce to light-up kindness in these difficult situations in our social relationships.

1. **Empathize**.
2. **Avoid** blame games.
3. **Forgive** and let go.

Empathy

Sympathy is where we understand others' negative feelings while we also become part of that emotion. If I cry along with my friend, that is a display of sympathy.

Empathy is where we genuinely feel for the other person, yet we do not become emotional prey. In this instance, I would not cry, yet I would stay with him, holding his hand, trying to help him recover.

The real mastery of empathy is supported by the practice of mindfulness, which I will explain later in this book.

Avoid Blame Games

It is natural for people to behave irrationally when they feel strong negative emotions. They lose logical reasoning and often blame others.

It is okay to accept that undue blame. Imagine if your friend offers you a book that you have no desire to read. Just pretend you like the book. Accept it, but do not commit to reading it.

Forgive and Let Go

Forgiving is a divine quality. Take every effort to forgive the other person, then let go of the terrible memories.

The lesson here is: do not defend. However, do not allow the blame to make you feel guilty. Maintain your positive emotions without being affected by the emotional insanity pointed at you. At the same time, aim to settle the other party's feelings involved without causing injury.

Such conflicts are not uncommon in our life. Still, by applying the right techniques, we can stabilize our kindness to maintain light-up.

22
FAIL SUCCESSFULLY

When everything goes against you, there is a message in it.

Embrace failure!

Failure is a dangerous storm that can turn off your kindness candle. Not many people in modern society are ready to forgive failure. When you experience it, then it is not uncommon for those who surround you to suddenly disappear from your life.

This situation is especially true in business, where failure is practically a death sentence. In real life, however, failure is an integral part of success. In my life's journey, I have been in countless situations where I encountered failure before achieving success.

I was hitting the point of bankruptcy in the fourth year of building the Social Enterprise, Sarvodaya-Fusion. The technology which we thought would allow us to become champions turned us broke. Cash flows dried up, and every effort

I made as founder resulted in the destruction of my team's motivation.

In desperation, I started searching for inspiration. I found two issues of *Harvard Business Review* magazines dedicated to the topic of failure.

It was an exceptional learning experience to read that people openly talk about failures, even in the business world!

Shortly after, I discovered a community in the USA that celebrated failure. These communities organize events called 'Fail Fairs,' and I contacted them to understand their unique concept.

Here is an excerpt from their literature:

"Let's discover the hidden lessons in failure. We understand failure is hard. Yet there is a grace in failure when you discover the underlying root causes. We will teach you techniques to uncover them. Well, here is the bonus. We will show you how to make fun out of failure."

Fun is essential!

Discovering fun inside failure was fascinating. The technique involved five steps.

- Find a good listener with a kind heart.
- Explain the failure until you lose the bitter feeling attached to it.
- Carry out a detailed postmortem analysis into the events leading to the failure.
- Search for a hidden gem inside the failure sequence that can inspire fun. (Trust me, it is always there).
- Prepare a presentation combining the story of failure and the hidden funny drama.

It is incredible how you can discover fun inside these failure stories. Try it!

Organizers qualified my presentation and invited me to the forthcoming Fail Fair in London. I was among the ten presenters lined up to present to around one hundred attendees — so-called 'failure stars.' That night, my presentation ended up being the third best.

The event had boosted my self-confidence so that I could talk about my failure publicly—the ability to break away from the grip of shame and fear. During the following months, I found the path to success again.

Failure is a part of success. It is an opportunity to learn the missing ingredients. Learn to fail successfully and then convert it to success.

The critical lesson in life is that if you want to succeed, never stop at failure. Keep exploring to learn the lessons hidden deep inside the failure; then, at the killer hour, always remind yourself the next stop is a success. And then keep going.

Grit and fortitude are necessary qualities you should endeavor to develop. They bring a deeper power to the Kindness Code's 'Be-Kind-to-You-First' principle. These qualities will support light-up kindness to eventually build robustness in you, where you can then achieve prosperity in life.

23
DARE TO DREAM

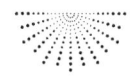

"This is the only thing I can share with you, my son. Please accept my humble gift... I am so proud of you," he hugged me tight, then started crying. He was one of the poorest in my large circle of relatives. Poverty probably made him less confident to talk; he was a silent man. Today, my success in entering university inspired him, and my aspirations sparked energy in him to speak up and share the pride.

Aspirations are like oxygen to fuel our life. Strong aspiration stays and gives us a reason to wake up in the morning and keep running day after day. They provide a platform to integrate our hopes and infuse energy.

As explained in Maslow's Hierarchy of Needs, aspirations enable us to achieve self-esteem and build confidence and pride.

Such qualities often bond relationships. Your aspiration becomes a shared dream by other loved ones by having you at its center. They will help you cheer your success, or even share a tear if you fail.

Thus, this space is where lighting your candle helps to light candles in others.

As a child, I had a big dream to become a medical doctor, a common aspiration shared by other family members. I felt it was a responsibility to harness my strengths to make everyone happy.

Then again, aspirations inherit a lifecycle by having a start, execution, and an end. It is crucial to continue through each of these phases to hit success.

When you master the art, you can ignite kindness at each phase to maintain motivation, navigate through failures, manage conflicts, and arrive at the sweet destination of success.

My dream to become a medical doctor shattered into pieces when I gained miserable AS exam results. That day, I saw my mother crying and my father speechless. I felt the gravity of the failure. It was excruciating.

Yet, my aspiration builder was powerful, so I soon developed a new aspiration. I opted to aim for a science degree — this time more closely related to my capabilities. I worked hard, and in the following year, I achieved the required grades.

My parents were so proud. We had a family celebration visiting my university in the beautiful city of Kandy on the Sri Lankan hillside. Many of my relatives joined the party. For the first time, some of them reached out to me privately, saying they were proud because I achieved something that they could not. That was the day the poorest uncle in my circle of relatives opened up. I felt so happy because I thought I could light their candles.

Aspirations are a good sign that we are kind to ourselves; to satisfy our basic needs of food, health, and shelter — a sign that a powerful network of relationships feeds our psychosocial needs. We dare to dream and have the drive to make them materialize. Success breeds success.

These aspirations drive us to prosperity in the mundane world, and they elevate us as qualified individuals. They serve two purposes; to light-up kindness in you, and to radiate kindness to others, which I will explain later. They enable sharing kindness between 'me' and 'them' toward prosperity.

24

LAW OF ATTRACTION

"Rising stars dream big," I cheered Jenny when she said she decided to do an MBA. Working as a small-business advisor in a Kent-based company, Jenny wanted to expand her career prospects.

She was a lovely young woman, full of energy. As her friend, I agreed to help her decide the right university, work out her finances, and find accommodation. We met regularly to share exciting stories about her student life, the lessons she learned, and how they inspired her work. Subjects such as financial accounting were not her forte, so I became a tutor to help.

One year later, balancing work and student life became strenuous for her. Life quickly became complicated, with Jenny becoming a victim to bullying. The lack of support around her, coupled with the pressure enforced by the impending exams, resulted in Jenny seeking support from university counsel.

Her persistence paid off, and she reached the last stage of MBA — the thesis. Months went by researching and writing the thesis while having parallel discussions with her supervisor. One day, she came to me furious.

"My supervisor is a real mess. He keeps changing his goals every day. I think he has some personal problems, that complicates his judgments on my project's arguments," she had told me.

"You know, Jenny. I faced the same problem in three countries. Repeatedly. Can you imagine?" I empathized and explained the personal struggles I experienced whilst completing my degrees.

These conflicts are common to any type of aspiration, education, career, business, and so on. Applying kindness is fundamental to manage such conflicts. Yet again, I found another helpful tool to light-up kindness in this complex territory. And I found it by accident.

Some time ago, I had to seek counselling from a friend when I was in dire straits. He introduced a twenty-minute long YouTube video titled, *"The Secret,"* which was my first ever introduction to the world-renowned philosophy *"Law of Attraction."* I watched it again and again. This led to the fail-fair story that I explained in a previous section and allowed me to recover from the failure.

"If you need anything, just ask it from the universe; believe that you will receive it, and live as if you have received it." That is the essence of the *Law of Attraction*.

Initially, I wasn't eager to subscribe to this philosophy because it did not emphasize the importance of qualities such as effort and determination to fulfill aspirations. William George Jordan says, in his famous book *The Power of*

Truth, "Living in an air castle is about as profitable as owning a half-interest in a rainbow." His writing continues to say, "Ambition, when added to tireless energy, is a great thing and a good thing, but it amounts too little in itself. Man cannot raise himself to higher things by what he would like to accomplish. To be of value, Ambition must ever be made manifest in zeal, in determination, in energy consecrated to an ideal."

Combining the valiant effort with the *Law of Attraction*, I recognize the pattern and how it could relate to my life's success stories since childhood.

When I was a poor child, having a bicycle was one of my biggest dreams. It started as a dire need to support my long walks under the scorching sun to help my parents. Then I started to enjoy daydreaming about a bicycle (my 'ask' in the *Law of Attraction* terminology). It had become such a joy; I used to run over the dusty roads for hours as if I were riding a bicycle (that was the 'receive'). I moved my legs like peddles, and my mind was absolutely doubtless. It was strange, but my joy of living in that dream was powerful enough to make me 'believe' in it.

Within months, I received a bicycle as a gift from someone unexpected. Clearly I didn't know at the time, but that was the first taste of success from my daydreaming. I have adopted this lesson to many following events in my life. Over the years, as my mastery has expanded, I would attract a foreign scholarship. Though I set the dream to go to Russia to receive my higher education, there was a slight twist — I ended up in Japan as a scholar, and the time taken to secure it was a few years longer than I expected.

You may face constant challenges when chasing big aspirations. These are often complex and unfamiliar, and some will also be beyond your control. Even worse, they manifest at a very rapid speed.

The *Law of Attraction* model offers a way to apply a positive mindset during those manifestations. It could help consistently ignite and light up kindness throughout the leading stages to arrive at the desired destination — success.

As you will note in the following sections, the Kindness Code's Step 3: Radiating kindness would help further in this process.

RADIATE

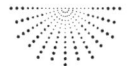

Kindness as a **Way of Living**
with
Right **Judgement**,
Decision Making, and
Virtue.

Feeling Complete Every Moment.

Ignite → Light-up → **Radiate**

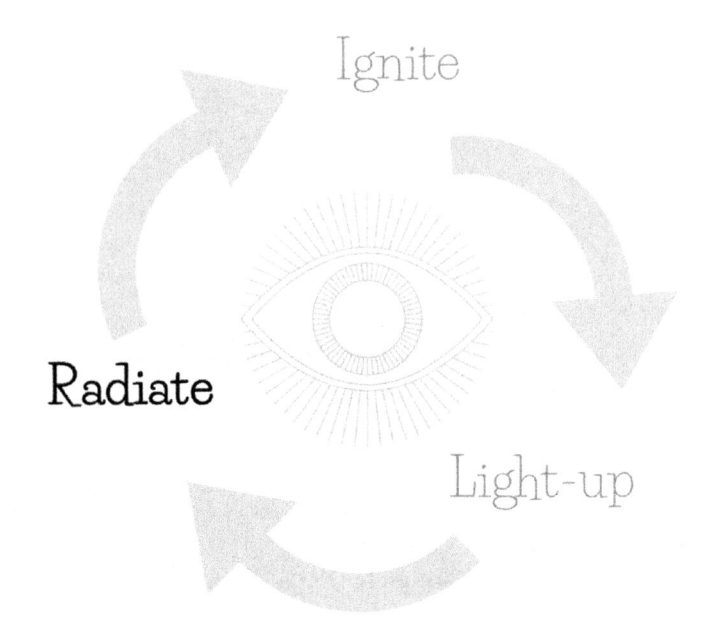

25
RADIATE KINDNESS

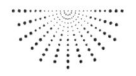

Just imagine the beauty of thousands of candles surrounding you. Imagine children, young and old, women and men holding these candles, their faces aglow. Now imagine it all started from the candle you are holding, and you are standing in the center with your shining candle.

Welcome to the state of radiate kindness.

Imagine if you could live with this shining candle every day.

Kindness is a way of living your life, enjoying ample happiness, and then radiating your kindness with many others. In that kinder life, you are beautifully connected with the entire universe. It is mutually enriching, elevating, and empowering.

It is a new paradigm that will require the right judgment, appropriate decision-making, and virtuous living. That way, kindness can guide you to live moment by moment with a feeling of fulfillment.

LET ME EXPLAIN HOW TO DO THIS.

You have developed a brighter and healthier individual in building your inner positive energy by being kind to yourself with ignite and light up. Now you are strong to stand up against the odds. The candle is strong to stand against storms. It is time to check whether the person in front of you has a candle or if it is still not lit. How can you radiate the light from your candle to make it brighter?

Here is where you give altruism its due place in your heart. You may break away from self-centeredness for your greater good and that of others. You recognize, respect, and engage with the inclusiveness, becoming a conscious part of the laws of interdependence.

WHY DO WE NEED TO RADIATE?

When excessive greed controls our aspirations, we lose our vision. We seek more and chase more, so we lose more of what we have achieved.

Unfortunately, most people only recognize this situation after hitting rock bottom. Disasters such as accidents, relationship breakdowns, critical illnesses, or even the death of a loved one topple us into dark places.

In my case, the domino effect of a combined set of breakdowns, my parents' deaths, my baby daughter's heart surgery, and the collapse of my first business all happening in a short space of time left me feeling annihilation right around me. That was devastating.

Why do we leave room to lose our hard-earned success? Let us learn to preserve it. With radiate, you can transcend happiness and prosperity to fulfillment.

. . .

Here comes **Principle #2: Be Kind to Others**.

The techniques introduced in the following sections will help you master the art of radiating kindness.

26
ANT & ME: LOVE & KINDNESS

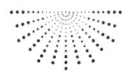

The tropical forest is not silent; it is filled with chirping birds, buzzing insects, squeaking monkeys, and grunting wild boars that build an orchestra of sound. Random rain showers create an energetic commotion in slow-flowing rivers. Sun, moon, and rains shift the chorus and melodies of this living world. There is a distinct serenity inside this symphony. The dark shades of giant tree canopies heighten this serenity, adding a layer of sogginess. Inside this secular nature's blanket, my mind settles into meditation. It awakens wisdom.

Escaping from blood-sucking leeches crawling on my bare foot was tough enough. Then, noticing scorpions falling from tree canopies after heavy rain and the sudden arrival of a wild boar locking its watchful eyes onto mine added to the trouble. It was ghastly, and I was scared to step out of my rudimentary cottage. I did not know how to respond to the unexpected hazards inside this forest.

I was in my first ever meditation retreat in the thick jungle, under my guru. As days went by, wisdom through meditation replaced fear with peace and harmony. With that, I could stroll barefoot, aware of the surroundings. I even mastered the art of brushing away an occasional leach before advancing beyond my ankles. When I touched them, I sensed a life beneath the ugliness.

We built this peaceful relationship around mutual respect. One day, I mindfully settled down in the riverbank to take a bath. Dragonflies usually occupied the rock I used to leave my towel and soap. But that day, a large colony of ants dominated the whole place, infesting the rock.

A closer look revealed thousands of them, some carrying eggs, while others busy taking food, pollen, decaying leaves, and even broken pieces of another insect. When I moved my fingers through the colony, a few ants defended. Then one ant came closer and started walking over my fingers. I had found a friend.

My perspectives about these insects had changed. I recognized the desire and struggle beneath it. Desire and struggle are common to every living organism. Then there is the concept of coexistence.

Everyone, including ants, is busy with their life's mission. We depend on limited resources around us, such as water, sunlight, trees, and air. When the ant and I met at the riverbank, we compete or share for these limited resources. When we choose to share, we form a healthy relationship, and we find peace and harmony.

The following morning was full of surprises; the ant colony was not there. Instead, one ant roamed around, holding a sizeable piece of food bigger than her entire body, in her tiny mandibles. As I approached, she started dancing all over the rock. Coming closer, she dropped this morsel over my fingers; she had brought a gift.

Ant and I both fell in love. We both found the energy of love inside our hearts, and that educated both parties greatly. Love guided us to respect each other and form friendship and bonds.

We both started radiating kindness toward each other.

At that point, I felt that even the river has a life. It shared its love and kindness to both the ant and me.

27

MEETING WITH A TERRORIST LEADER

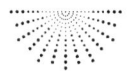

2002, Sri Lanka.

I felt horror in every step. The blood-red eyes were like laser beams targeted at me. Lust for killing was written in those eyes. The loaded machine guns they held were more significant than their bodies wearing over-sized tiger-striped khaki uniforms. I was at the entry point to the land governed by the gruesome terrorist group known as LTTE. The land was hot, dry, and dusty. They had fought a bloody war on this land for over three decades, seeking an independent state called Tamil Eelam in North Eastern Sri Lanka.

The goal of my visit was to negotiate the office space to execute humanitarian activities for Sarvodaya, the national charity I served back then. My office staff had spent months to get approval from both government authorities and terrorist command. It took five hours over bumpy roads to arrive here.

The office we arrived at was different in its outlook compared to the entry post — orderly and quiet. A soldier directed us into an outside summer hut, where the meeting took place. During the next twenty minutes, before the leader joined the meeting, three of his assistants arrived one by one. They sat in random seats, disregarding me. I tried to open a conversation to clear the tension in the air, but they were unwelcoming, instead shielding further into the brutality of silence.

Sitting in the stealthy silence, I closely observed those people sitting around. Behind the khaki dress and black shoes, I felt humanness. *"They do breathe as I do, though they speak a different language. There must be some form of kindness inside them. They may have families, too, I silently assured myself."*

Finally, the leader arrived hastily and sat in the vacant central seat. Right behind him, mounted on the wall, was a framed photo of their famous LTTE leader, standing with a commanding posture. Without any greeting, he started preaching, "Let me remind you, this is our territory. We earned every inch by beating your lousy army, under the command of our leader. Make no mistake — we are winning…This is our land… you have to obey the rules set by our command."

His voice was deep, commanding, and directed to instill fear. Mostly referring to the battles they won since 1983, the expansion of their territory from North to East since then, and their suicide cadres' commitment. He frequently referred to the names of fallen Generals in government command and how their heroic commanders outplayed those historical battles. In his train of commanding preach, he had left no room to open conversation to the humanitarian side — poverty, health, and safety of the mothers and

THE KINDNESS CODE

children affected by the raging war. In his eyes, they were only material that could be utilized for a single purpose; that is, to win their land. I could not find any space in which to plant a seed of kindness.

Yet, inside hopelessness, I had found hope. The candle inside me was strong amidst battling winds. And the inner voice reminded me, *"This is another human leader. He is on a mission, working hard to win his battle. There must be some common ground to explore somewhere."* For one long hour, I kept listening to him with empathy while radiating kindness toward him.

There was a small but noticeable pause after he finished. I started slowly but confidently. My inner candle started to radiate more. Instead of the current affairs, I started exploring common ground reminding him of the history through my childhood memories. I told him about visiting the Northern region where I admired the colorful Hindu temples, the joy of taking part in harvesting then-famous onion cultivations, and the stories my parents told me about shared labor between communities for generations.

His eyes became smaller, and his face brighter. I had found a path in which to shine the light on his childhood memories, which were long-forgotten by the brutality of leadership demands in the battlefront. I opted not to discuss the official matters, yet laid the groundwork to build a healthy relationship. We agreed to set the next meeting date to start conversations between his ground leaders and my ground staff.

During the next visit, he served me and my team lunch, where I recalled stories by Mahathma Gandhi and Nelson Mandela, and how they had given leadership to millions, yet through non-violent means. Our conversation was peaceful and open-minded, and he acknowledged the importance of humanitarian work to affected communities.

Toward the end, my kindness could find the softer side of that leader. We became colleagues with a common objective to serve the underserved. Months later, they approved opening our office so that we could deliver humanitarian support to affected communities, including children and mothers.

28

KIND STRANGERS IN THE GLOBAL
VILLAGE

In the early days of global travel, my destinations were to less-developed nations. As the flight landed in a new airport, the travel adventure dissipated, and the glee of being in a new environment wore off as I stepped out of the terminal building. I felt anxious and often disoriented by being unable to understand the nuances of facial expressions, appearance, and behavior of the communities I met.

How could I find a hotel? Could I trust these taxi drivers? They looked reckless, hasty, and often unruly. Inside, the taxi smells were unsettling. Colors, fractured shop fronts, and dusty decadent streets were different and depressing. Then came the food, spices, drinks, and the whole gamut of strange things daunting the nostalgia. The cultural shock was not pleasant.

I later discovered the baby steps to radiate kindness when building relationships. It started with a long, healthy conversation with the taxi driver, the first person I met outside the airport. Many drivers used to mount a photo of their loved ones, or else religious figures, and I would take that as the point of conversation.

That would gradually expand to learn more about their family, daily lifestyle, religious beliefs, cultural knots, and other topics. Radiating kindness could help me build friendships with strangers quickly and reduce my stress significantly.

When I visited rural villages in India or Nepal, language barriers became a significant challenge because they were often illiterate. Then I learned the power of the smile; that will connect anywhere at any time with many human beings. A smile can break down barriers of unfamiliarity or discomfort, instantly opening to diverse forms of conversations, sharing tea, sign language, or broken English, bringing even more smiles. Radiating kindness was beautiful; thus, it has become the norm that when I leave them, we share gifts and often shed tears. That was the indication of the universal bond that kindness enabled to develop between strangers.

One day, I traveled to an international gathering in Harare, the capital of Zimbabwe. Back then, Zimbabwe was sadly known for notorious corruption and poverty. The scary news about Zimbabwe hung in my head when my flight landed. The airport pickup arranged by Dutch organizers of the gathering was a great consolation to me.

It was around 5 p.m., and dusk fell as we drove down a dusty road full of potholes. Flocks of animals and people carrying large bundles of logs passed along the way. Some women carried babies on their backs and loads on their heads. The honking of the driver's horn was loud, overriding the engine roar of the old Mercedes-Benz car in which we rode. I sat in the back seat with two fellow travelers from the Caribbean

Islands and Morocco. The third traveler, a lady from Botswana, had settled into the front seat.

A few miles into the drive, we got into an accident. Though none of us was injured, the vehicle was damaged, and the engine stopped responding. A burst of angry words started between two drivers, and then we saw our driver lose his claims as the other driver left the scene. Desperate and lost, our driver instructed us to stay on the road and disappeared to find help, leaving the car in the middle of the road.

Loaded buses and vans quickly dashed around the broken car, and one reckless driver almost hit our baggage as his speeding van bumped into a deep pothole. "I hear a lot about a mugging in this country," the lady from Botswana finally broke the silence as vigilant eyes in those overloaded vehicles marked us.

With darkness falling and no-where to go, the four of us stood outside on the dusty road, which was surrounded by trees and bushes; there were no streetlamps.

"Are there wild animals in this area?" the gentleman from the Caribbean Islands wondered about the bushes in the roadside. Everyone drew closer to each other with each random question, like a helpless flock of birds settling into darkness. My kindness candle was strong enough to rise to the challenge and to make them feel comfortable. I opened a water bottle and shared some emergency snacks left in my bag. Everyone responded to the gesture of kindness as it brought some sense of mutual trust and security, though still, they kept silent.

The driver later returned with a triumphant smile. We were finally dropped at the hotel safely. The next morning, Botswana lady joined me at the breakfast table with a broad smile on her face. "Thank you for those biscuits... I don't know... I felt something special. You know, I was so scared. Anything could have happened to us there."

Kindness has the magical power to bring safety and security into our lives, even in unfamiliar places. It breaks down the wall of difference between strangers and helps us discover the hidden divine inside us. It elevates us into a higher plane, which makes us, at times, feel supernatural. That's why radiating kindness is magical!

29
KINDNESS AS A WAY OF LIFE

Let me dedicate my life today,
to the care of those who come my way.
Let me touch each one with a healing hand,
and the gentle art for which I stand.
And then tonight when the day is done,
O, let me rest in peace if I helped just one!

This poem was stuck to the sidewall of a fridge, a comfortable chair facing it. A doctor I once knew would come home at the end of the day and sit here, reflecting on her day full of kindness.

This doctor held a magic wand in her hand. In her specialty, she regularly executed one of the most painful medical procedures — bone marrow testing. Yet, the power of her magic wand was such that she carried out these procedures with a kindness and skill that her patients felt little pain.

This story is an example of how one can radiate kindness to the world in everyday life. It is how kindness plays as a way of life.

Such beautiful events can occur in philanthropy, social enterprising, for-profit enterprises, or any profession. If you look at it this way, industry and working places are the channels in which to deliver your skills to serve someone else. They are trading places, where we transact our skills, services, or products with others, and each trading place has an end recipient.

Try to connect with that end recipient. Here are three simple steps to do that:

1. Imagine the **end recipient**.
2. Feel **the experience** of that recipient.
3. Do your best to **enhance** that experience.

When I served at the largest charity, Sarvodaya in Sri Lanka, part of my work involved authorizing community projects. The authorization meant I signed piles of printed documents while sitting at the head office's reasonably comfortable room. Before placing my signature, I would seek details from my staff that enabled me to visualize the end recipients: the faces of orphans, smiling mothers, and children playing at village kindergartens. Often, I recalled the community songs celebrating their long-awaited entry road to their village. Those images ignited my kindness and light-up my spirit to radiate kindness with the seal of my signature.

As I explained in previous sections, every transaction is an action originating from thought and emotion. When we ignite kindness in our thought process, it enables compassion to decorate every transaction.

Therefore, it follows that if you make cupcakes, they will be delicious when wrapped in kindness. If you write books, the words will have an extra touch of kindness. If you are a farmer, plumber, accountant, lawyer, software engineer, or any other professional, your every single act will make a big difference. The recipients of those services and products will feel that.

Yet, how do we maintain our kindness in every moment that we pass throughout the day? You will find the answer in the next section.

30
MINDFULNESS

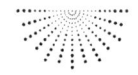

We start the day with a bright mind, but that brightness erodes when the events become complicated as the day evolves. Maintaining our kindness through those negative corridors is tough. Mindfulness is a brilliant technique in which to help you navigate through those tough moments.

> "Waking up this morning, I smile. Twenty-four brand new hours are before me. I vow to live fully in each moment and to look at all beings with eyes of compassion."
>
> — THICH NHAT HANH

Rev. Thich Nhat Hanh is a great teacher who has introduced mindfulness to the world. As I began to learn mindfulness, I started with his famous book, *Peace is Every Step*. To pay my great respect to this teacher, I took the liberty to pick a few memorable quotes from his life of work and elaborate in this section.

> "Life is available only in the present. That is why we should walk in such a way that every step can bring us to the here and the now."
>
> — THICH NHAT HANH

Mindfulness is all about 'awareness.' It is about 'Training Mind' to be aware of 'What our body is doing.' Every work by our body can be simplified into three things — walk, stand, or sit.

It is that simple. Yet, we lose this simplicity in the absence of awareness. Mindfulness involves:

- **Learning** what awareness is.
- **Developing** awareness skills.
- **Maintaining** awareness in crucial activities where we walk, stand, or sit.

The goal here is to train your mind to cease overthinking. Stay focused on the present moment, and bring your attention to it again and again.

> "The mind can go in a thousand directions, but on this beautiful path, I walk in peace. With each step, the wind blows. With each step, a flower blooms."
>
> — THICH NHAT HANH

Our senses are the windows to the world. They consistently connect with nature and other surrounding events to generate emotions. Sometimes, we learn to close the windows to avoid blowing wind and scorching sun and to maintain ambiance. Mindfulness is the only way in which to secure that ambiance; the sustainability of a positive mind.

> "When we are mindful, deeply in touch with the present moment, our understanding of what is going on deepens, and we begin to be filled with acceptance, joy, peace, and love."
>
> — THICH NHAT HANH

This way, mindfulness helps you sustain a positive mind, ignite kindness, light-up, and radiate kindness to live life as a way of kindness.

31
DEATH

"We are walking a tightrope with death on either side," the deep voice of Will Smith narrating directly to the camera appears through a black and white close-up in the famous movie, *One Strange Rock*; a cinematic National Geographic documentary. This particular episode explains the miraculous formation of the planet Earth and how it can positively change our perspective on death.

"Death is a necessary evil for us to live our life on this planet earth." The deep voice continues, with a scenic explanation of death's natural cycle — how the dead body becomes a sumptuous feast for maggots and micro-organisms. The corpse's muscles, tissues, and bones are gradually transformed into granular minerals and nutrients. The plant roots grow deeper into the soil to absorb these minerals and systematically combine with the energy trapped from sunshine through photosynthesis. We love the product — flowers and fruits. We need living creatures to grow, once again, forming muscles, tissues, and bones in the living body. With death and birth, the cycle continues.

Death is nature's cycle to sustain us all, from plants to living beings. It promotes inter-dependence and refreshes life. When we recognize this nature of impermanence, it dissipates our fear of death and empowers us to live with reality and respect.

I had a rare opportunity to comprehend this reality, which has transpired my perspective into life.

On one gray Autumn morning in the UK, I got a phone call informing me that my guru had passed away. One month later, I visited the monastery in Sri Lanka to pay my last respects. As per his last wish, fellow monks had placed his body in a secured cave in the solitary jungle within twenty-four hours. Advanced meditation practitioners could visit to contemplate impermanence by observing his decaying body. I was among the privileged few to visit this mystic cave.

Fear of seeing a decaying dead body prompted hesitation. Yet, in contemplating my guru's exemplary intentions to exhibit his own decaying body, I found courage.

I felt sick with creeping apprehension as I silently followed the monk as he guided me to the cave. The walking footpath was narrow, appearing like a dark tunnel covered by dense vegetation of ferns and small trees, competing under huge ghostly canopies. Stepping over layers of damp leaves, I felt growing distress and a mounting heartbeat. A few minutes through the woods, we arrived at a large white rock surrounded by a wounded patch of virgin forest. Husky black ants and shiny-orange-colored bugs were rebuilding their broken colonies in random places.

A horizontal wooden door barricaded the tomb built into the rock. The monk put the key into a padlock, holding the door at the upper end. It was tight, and he had to make an effort to unlock it. The door opened downward with a loud cry, revealing the tomb, tightly covered by a thick glass wall. A thin sunbeam penetrated from a cavity, backlighting the tomb space.

The decaying body lay in the center. It was just lying over the naked rock surface. Its appearance was that of decaying wood covered by a yellow robe. I failed to recognize the complete body. Finally, I spotted his face — growing moss covered it entirely. His eyes and nose were not visible in that moss ball protruding from the yellow robe, yet, his open mouth was noticeable. A maggot danced between the jaws.

"This is the body of my guru." Instead of any sadness or fear, I felt emptiness. That feeling grew more significant and profound, taking me to my knees and bending my head as I worshipped the decaying body.

At that moment, I was awakened to the phenomena of impermanence (i.e. *anithya*) — the shadow behind our life. The wisdom it has cultivated gradually grew, uprooting the obsession of self, searching for exuberant tastes, aspiring to build empires and a legacy of 'Me.' The power of simplicity tiptoed into my mind, settling down to form a deep sense of mindful living, tapping into loving-kindness and altruistic joy at that very moment called 'Now.'

This understanding tremendously empowered my ability to radiate kindness to other living beings.

32
SELF-TRANSCENDENCE

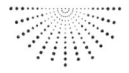

> "Content is the greatest wealth."
>
> — LORD BUDDHA.

We lose the feeling of content when we obsess with 'self:' self-identity, self-esteem, self-improvement, and so on. Paul Thagard, a Canadian philosopher and cognitive scientist, argues that the self is a complex system operating at four different levels; molecular, neural, psychological, and social. In our endless pursuit to satisfy this self at all these levels, we lose content.

Abraham Maslow explains in his famous *Hierarchy of Needs* that the pursuit of personal satisfaction begins by fulfilling the basic needs of food, water, and shelter. Upon satisfying basic needs, the quest progresses upward in the pyramid of hierarchy to fulfill safety, then searching for love and self-esteem, and, finally, toward self-actualization — the realization of one's full potential.

However, though self-serving self-actualization is presented as a worthy development goal, Maslow subsequently introduced transcendence as the most honorable goal in which to pursue.

Transcendence means rising above the 'self' and relating to something 'above the self.' Maslow writes, "Transcendence refers to the very highest and most inclusive or holistic levels of human consciousness, behaving and relating, as ends rather than means, to oneself, to significant others, to human beings in general, to other species, to nature, and the cosmos."

Courtney Ackerman, author, and researcher of positive psychology, explains four characteristics of transcended:

1. A shift in focus from the **self** to others.
2. A shift in **values**.
3. An increase in **moral** concern.
4. Emotions of **elevation**.

A shift in focus from the self to others – this shift from selfishness to consideration of others' needs is an essential feature of self-transcendence.

A shift in values – those who have achieved self-transcendence no longer find themselves driven by external rewards, but by intrinsic motivation driven by morals and values. They will often find the activity itself as the reward.

An increase in moral concern – Holding to principles of right behavior becomes a defining aspect of self-transcended.

Emotions of elevation – Positive emotions, such as feeling uplifted, feeling elevated, awe and amazement, are characterized in self-transcended life.

In her article in *Positive Psychology*, Courtney further writes, "If you know anyone who is constantly working to meet the needs of less fortunate others, who are driven not by money or rewards but by an internal drive and is always concerned with doing the right thing, you likely have an example of self-transcendence right in front of you!"

I found one example in Dr. A. T. Ariyaratne, also known as Little Gandhi among his peers, in Sri Lanka. He exemplifies self-transcended leaders with whom I had the privilege to closely associate. Starting life as a simple school teacher, he has dedicated his life to serving deprived communities. During the country's raging civil war, he has led peace meditations across the country, radiating kindness across hundreds of thousands. The Sarvodaya, meaning awakening of all in Sanskrit and the most significant charitable movement founded by him in Sri Lanka, is well-known for serving millions across the country over six decades. Under his leadership, numerous leaders recognized self-transcendence using the means of spirituality and humanitarian engagement to serve the underserved. Sarvodaya is one excellent example of institutionalizing kindness into the organization.

Though it is common to find well-known personalities such as Nelson Mandela, Mahatma Gandhi, and the Dalai Lama as self-transcended individuals, according to Maslow, anyone can reach self-transcendence.

Pierre Jones, a simple man and a friend who earned my respect for the remarkable, humble life he lives, believes that radiating kindness is not random; he dedicates his volunteer energy managing a small charity based in the UK to support disadvantaged communities in Ethiopia. He also recently set up a small business to help his brother. During summer, he cultivates a small vegetable allotment. When I walk with him in Faversham's small town, many villagers stop by to greet this little man with a big heart. Inspired by all his work, I requested a page of his kindness diary.

- Rescued a caterpillar stranded on a path and took it somewhere where it could live.
- Found slugs on the allotment and rather than killing them, put them on the compost heap.
- Spoke with Jimmy, the homeless person who lives in a wood, and listened to him, even though he spoke angrily.
- Listened to a lady in a charity shop and let her talk about looking after her elderly mother and father. She said she wasn't bad for getting angry with them, but instead, she was just tired and worn out because of having to care for them.
- Went and gave Mum some French beans from my allotment.
- Picked up rubbish along the creek.
- Rang my friend, who was due to have a check for bowel cancer today.

Look at the diversity of those simple acts. Digging a little deeper into those acts, you may notice altruism plays a dominant role in his daily life. Kindness is radiated to family, society, and the entire eco-system of living associated with his life.

These living examples, from renowned leaders to simple individuals, have one thing in common — they found self-fulfillment in abundance. Anyone can achieve transcendence. It enables one to live with simplicity and virtues without compromising the aspirations of modern life. It will help define your 'ideal self' and live life as a happy and productive individual who finds health and well-being in living by virtue of kindness.

Radiating kindness helps to find the Zen of now and enjoy the miracle of existence within the ever-unfolding dance of the universe. This will momentarily self-transcend to a higher purpose in life.

> "Loving-kindness generates kindness, that leads to altruistic joy."
>
> — LORD BUDDHA.

33
MEDITATION

Meditation is a journey with our minds!

It starts with awareness and continues by acquiring wisdom, then moving to explore the human mind's hidden power. Meditation is the most helpful tool I have found that can radiate kindness toward achieving the status of transcendence.

Meditation brings:

- Better **focus**.
- Less anxiety and **stress**.
- More **creativity**.
- Better **memory**.
- Youthful **feeling**.

Meditation is not necessarily religious; its origin has roots in almost every religion in the world. The modern world has ascribed it to nearly anything, from physical fitness to mental health and stress management. Meditation has many forms.

From the perspective of Buddhist meditation practices (which I learned and spent the best part of the last 25 years of my life practicing), meditation can be organized into three basic types:

1. *Anapana* (Breathing).
2. *Metta* (loving-kindness).
3. *Vipassana* (insight).

With transcendence as a goal, these meditations will take your mind through the journey in three stages:

1. **Sathi** - mind enters into a state where the meditator knows almost everything that the body does.
2. **Samadhi** - mind goes into a state of trance, where it reaches beyond the normal status of the mind-body continuum. It reaches a different level of power.
3. **Vipassana and higher levels of *Samadhi*** - the mind's higher power is used to explore the nature of body and mind, its existence, and inter-relations — even going to states beyond this life.

Mastering meditation is an excellent aspiration for one to have. One has to learn and follow the right steps to get the best from it.

Kindness Code is an easy way to apply kindness as a daily preparation in building a stable meditation practice. The three steps, ignite, light up, and radiate of the Kindness Code, are a way to apply kindness with the right understanding into what it is, how you use it, and why. Meditation is then the wisdom plane enabling you to combine all this kindness to achieve transcendence.

34
WHY KINDNESS CODE?

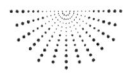

Congratulations, you have reached the destination for a new beginning.

You wanted to find solutions to these burning questions:

1. How to sustain **happiness**.
2. How to find the path to **prosperity**.
3. How to sustain success and **feel complete**.

You have learned about the Kindness Code, the three steps, and the two principles.

Ignite, light up, and radiate provide you a systematic path in which to apply kindness in incremental steps at the different stages in everyday life. They will help you maintain your motivation, positive mind, and focus.

The Code will help you organize your random acts of kindness. It will help you know when and how to be kind to yourself first, then friends, family, and others. This understanding will then enable you to apply kindness with clarity and find its true essence to elevate and empower you and others.

It will enable you to choose relevant tools, such as positive imagination, the law of attraction, mindfulness, and meditation, to support your aspirations. You will then be able to reach the ultimate goal of transcendence toward discovering a higher purpose in life.

THE KINDNESS CODE

Ignite

Radiate

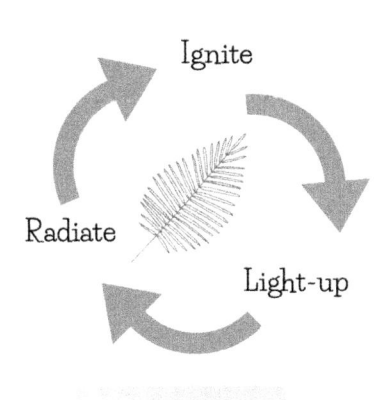

Light-up

Principle #1:
Be Kind to You First

Principle #2:
Be Kind to Others

Kindness Code

ACKNOWLEDGMENTS

The Kindness Code was a form of social innovation derived by combining the author's life experiences and meditation insights. This innovation process required verifying certain complex assumptions, such as energy relations between love and loving-kindness, and their direct influence on kindness. Evidence provided by Quantum research was not sufficient to establish such a relationship. Psychology research also did not provide enough clarity in which to interpret the aspects of emotions and thoughts concerning the *Nama-Rupa* (mental and physical) insights of Vipassana meditation.

I am grateful to the Hela Suwaya team for helping me to verify such complex assumptions. They helped organize direct conversations with advanced meditators and the supreme teacher Maitreya Bodhisattva. Such conversations enabled me to validate assumptions and triangulate my personal meditation insights.

Hela Suwaya is a registered charity / social enterprise in Sri Lanka promoting humanitarian work, serving thousands of impoverished communities. Their work involves delivering plant-based-medicines, organic food, and teaching Metta meditation under the direct guidance of Maitreya Bodhisattva.

Maitreya Bodhisattva is cited in Buddhist literature as the next Buddha in line, as a successor to the present Buddha, Gautama. In Sri Lanka, they display statues of Maitreya Bodhisattva in almost every major temple. Maitreya (also *Metta*) in Sanskrit means "loving-kindness," and it depicts the meditation techniques founded in loving-kindness under this Bodhisattva. Wikipedia explains how Maitreya has been adopted by many non-Buddhist religions such as the White Lotus New Religious movement. In Sri Lanka, Hela Suwaya works directly under the guidance of Maitreya Bodhisattva, where he was also referred to as God Natha.

Many people shared their kindness in making this book a reality. Among them, Priyantha Senanayake, Asini Liyanage, Savani Liyanage, and Devni Liyanage, Adam Jason Moore, Kerry Burgess deserve my more profound gratitude for the remarkable contributions they have made with their spirit.

BIBLIOGRAPHY

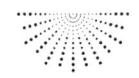

1. The Power of Positive Thinking. Johns Hopkins Medicine. https://www.hopkinsmedicine.org/health/wellness-and-prevention/the-power-of-positive-thinking. [Accessed 21 Aug 2020].
2. Motivation and personality. Maslow, A. H. (1954). New York: Harper and Row.
3. How Vulnerable Should You Let Yourself Be?, L. F. Seltzer, "Psychology Today," 03 Jan 2018. https://www.psychologytoday.com/gb/blog/evolution-the-self/201801/how-vulnerable-should-you-let-yourself-be [Accessed 20 Aug 2020].
4. Welcome to the Dare to Lead Hub! Brene Brown. https://daretolead.brenebrown.com/. [Accessed 20 Aug 2020].
5. The art of happiness: a handbook for living. Dalai Lama XIV & Howard C. Cutler, New York : Riverhead Books, 1998.
6. The devious art of lying by telling the truth, Melissa Hogenboom. Nov 2017. https://www.bbc.com/

future/article/20171114-the-disturbing-art-of-lying-by-telling-the-truth. [Accessed 20 Aug 2020].
7. The Power of Truth: Individual Problems and Possibilities. William George Jordan. 1902.
8. Peace Is Every Step: The Path of Mindfulness in Everyday Life. Thich Nhât, Hạnh, and Arnold Kotler. New York, N.Y: Bantam Books, 1991.
9. What Is the Self? Paul Thagard. "Psychology Today". June, 2014. https://www.psychologytoday.com/gb/blog/hot-thought/201406/what-is-the-self. [Accessed 20 Aug 2020].
10. What is Self-Transcendence? Definition and 6 Examples. Courtney Ackerman. June, 2020. "Positive Psychology" https://positivepsychology.com/self-transcendence/ . [Accessed 20 Aug 2020].
11. The farther reaches of human nature. Maslow, A. H. (1971). New York, NY, US: Arkana/Penguin Books.

ONE FINAL WORD

P.S. If you enjoyed this book, please drop me a line; I love reading your feedback.

Kindnesscode@gmail.com

And, then please leave it as a review. Reviews are the lifeblood to promote our mission. By doing so, you are contributing to the mission of making the world a kinder place.

Please choose the appropriate country link from the following list to leave the review.

- US: http://www.amazon.com/review/create-review?&asin=B08HZC8WXT
- UK: http://www.amazon.co.uk/review/create-review?&asin=B08HZC8WXT
- Canada: http://www.amazon.ca/review/create-review?&asin=B08HZC8WXT

- India: http://www.amazon.in/review/create-review?&asin=B08HZC8WXT
- Australia: http://www.amazon.com.au/review/create-review?&asin=B08HZC8WXT
- Netherlands: http://www.amazon.nl/review/create-review?&asin=B08HZC8WXT
- Denmark: http://www.amazon.de/review/create-review?&asin=B08HZC8WXT
- Japan: http://www.amazon.jp/review/create-review?&asin=B08HZC8WXT

Thank you.

Printed in Great Britain
by Amazon